In Their Words

Original Documents, Poetry, Stories,
and Hymns from World History

Edited by

Ray, Charlene, and John Notgrass

In Their Words is a compilation of original sources from world history that range from the Code of Hammurabi around 1750 BC to speeches by Ronald Reagan in the 1980s. It includes documents, speeches, excerpts from books, poems, short stories, fables, and fairy tales. A special feature are many hymns from 200 AD to the twentieth century. The materials in this volume introduce the reader to significant people and ideas that have helped to shape our world.

Cover Design by Charlene Notgrass
Graphic Design by Charlene and John Notgrass

Notgrass Company
370 South Lowe Avenue, Suite A
PMB 211
Cookeville, Tennessee 38501
1-800-211-8793
books@notgrass.com
www.notgrass.com

ISBN: 978-1-933410-38-8

Table of Contents

Excerpts from The Code of Hammurabi

(c. 1750 B.C.)

The following provisions are taken from the Code of Hammurabi. Comments are in brackets.

1. If any one ensnare another, putting a ban upon him, but he can not prove it, then he that ensnared him shall be put to death.

2. If any one bring an accusation of any crime before the elders, and does not prove what he has charged, he shall, if it be a capital offense charged, be put to death. [These provisions would discourage making false accusations.]

3. If any one bring an accusation against a man, and the accused go to the river and leap into the river, if he sink in the river his accuser shall take possession of his house. But if the river prove that the accused is not guilty, and he escape unhurt, then he who had brought the accusation shall be put to death, while he who leaped into the river shall take possession of the house that had belonged to his accuser. [This put the verdict in the hands of the river, since the people believed that the gods would administer justice fairly in this way.]

Inscription from the Code of Hammurabi written in cuneiform

4. If a judge try a case, reach a decision, and present his judgment in writing; if later error shall appear in his decision, and it be through his own fault, then he shall pay twelve times the fine set by him in the case, and he shall be publicly removed from the judge's bench, and never again shall he sit there to render judgment. [This made judges accountable for their decisions.]

5. If any one steal cattle or sheep, or an ass, or a pig or a goat, if it belong to a god or to the court, the thief shall pay thirtyfold therefore; if they belonged to a freed man of the king he shall pay tenfold; if the thief has nothing with which to pay he shall be put to death.

6. If any one take a male or female slave of the court, or a male or female slave of a freed man, outside the city gates, he shall be put to death.

7. If any one receive into his house a runaway male or female slave of the court, or of a freedman, and does not bring it out at the public proclamation of the major domus, the master of the house shall be put to death.

8. If any one break a hole into a house (break in to steal), he shall be put to death before that hole and be buried.

9. If any one is committing a robbery and is caught, then he shall be put to death.

10. If fire break out in a house, and someone who comes to put it out cast his eye upon the property of the owner of the house, and take the property of the master of the house, he shall be thrown into that self-same fire.

11. If a man rent his field for tillage for a fixed rental, and receive the rent of his field, but bad weather come and destroy the harvest, the injury falls upon the tiller of the soil.

12. If any one be too lazy to keep his dam in proper condition, and does not so keep it; if then the dam break and all the fields be flooded, then shall he in whose dam the break occurred be sold for money, and the money shall replace the corn which he has caused to be ruined.

13. If he be not able to replace the corn, then he and his possessions shall be divided among the farmers whose corn he has flooded.

14. If any one open his ditches to water his crop, but is careless, and the water flood the field of his neighbor, then he shall pay his neighbor corn for his loss.

100. If any one give another silver, gold, or anything else to keep, he shall show everything to some witness, draw up a contract, and then hand it over for safe keeping.

101. If he turn it over for safe keeping without witness or contract, and if he to whom it was given deny it, then he has no legitimate claim.

102. If any one leave his house, run away, and then his wife go to another house, if then he return, and wishes to take his wife back: because he fled from his home and ran away, the wife of this runaway shall not return to her husband.

103. If a man's wife, who lives in his house, wishes to leave it, plunges into debt, tries to ruin her house, neglects her husband, and is judicially convicted: if her husband offer her release, she may go on her way, and he gives her nothing as a gift of release. If her husband does not wish to release her, and if he take another wife, she shall remain as servant in her husband's house.

104. If a woman quarrel with her husband, and say: "You are not congenial to me," the reasons for her prejudice must be presented. If she is guiltless, and there is no fault on her part, but he leaves and neglects her, then no guilt attaches to this woman, she shall take her dowry and go back to her father's house.

105. If she is not innocent, but leaves her husband, and ruins her house, neglecting her husband, this woman shall be cast into the water.

106. If a man wish to put his son out of his house, and declare before the judge: "I want to put my son out," then the judge shall examine into his reasons. If the son be guilty of no great fault, for which he can be rightfully put out, the father shall not put him out.

107. If he be guilty of a grave fault, which should rightfully deprive him of the filial relationship, the father shall forgive him the first time; but if he be guilty of a grave fault a second time the father may deprive his son of all filial relation.

108. If a State slave or the slave of a freed man marry the daughter of a free man, and children are born, the master of the slave shall have no right to enslave the children of the free.

109. If an artisan has undertaken to rear (an adopted) child and teaches him his craft, he can not be demanded back (by the birth father).

110. If he has not taught him his craft, this adopted son may return to his father's house.

111. If a son strike his father, his hands shall be hewn off.

112. If a man put out the eye of another man, his eye shall be put out. [This and the following provisions embody the "eye for an eye" principle that appears in the Law of Moses also. Such laws discourage revenge; someone who has lost an eye is not permitted to destroy his attacker's entire family.]

113. If he break another man's bone, his bone shall be broken.

114. If he put out the eye of a freed man, or break the bone of a freed man, he shall pay one gold mina.

115. If he put out the eye of a man's slave, or break the bone of a man's slave, he shall pay one-half of its value.

116. If a man knock out the teeth of his equal, his teeth shall be knocked out. [A tooth for a tooth]

117. If any one strike the body of a man higher in rank than he, he shall receive sixty blows with an ox-whip in public.

118. If a free-born man strike the body of another free-born man of equal rank, he shall pay one gold mina.

119. If a freed man strike the body of another freed man, he shall pay ten shekels in money.

120. If the slave of a freed man strike the body of a freed man, his ear shall be cut off.

121. If during a quarrel one man strike another and wound him, then he shall swear, "I did not injure him wittingly," and pay the physicians.

122. If a physician make a large incision with an operating knife and cure it, or if he open a tumor (over the eye) with an operating knife, and saves the eye, he shall receive ten shekels in money.

123. If the patient be a freed man, he receives five shekels.

124. If he be the slave of some one, his owner shall give the physician two shekels.

125. If a physician make a large incision with the operating knife, and kill him, or open a tumor with the operating knife, and cut out the eye, his hands shall be cut off.

126. If a physician make a large incision in the slave of a freed man, and kill him, he shall replace the slave with another slave.

127. If a veterinary surgeon perform a serious operation on an ass or an ox, and cure it, the owner shall pay the surgeon one-sixth of a shekel as a fee.

128. If he perform a serious operation on an ass or ox, and kill it, he shall pay the owner one-fourth of its value.

129. If a builder build a house for some one and complete it, he shall give him a fee of two shekels in money for each sar of surface.

130. If a builder build a house for some one, and does not construct it properly, and the house which he built fall in and kill its owner, then that builder shall be put to death.

131. If it kill the son of the owner the son of that builder shall be put to death.

132. If it kill a slave of the owner, then he shall pay slave for slave to the owner of the house.

133. If it ruin goods, he shall make compensation for all that has been ruined, and inasmuch as he did not construct properly this house which he built and it fell, he shall re-erect the house from his own means.

134. If a builder build a house for some one, even though he has not yet completed it; if then the walls seem toppling, the builder must make the walls solid from his own means.

135. If a shipbuilder build a boat of sixty gur for a man, he shall pay him a fee of two shekels in money.

136. If a shipbuilder build a boat for some one, and do not make it tight, if during that same year that boat is sent away and suffers injury, the shipbuilder shall take the boat apart and put it together tight at his own expense. The tight boat he shall give to the boat owner.

137. If a man rent his boat to a sailor, and the sailor is careless, and the boat is wrecked or goes aground, the sailor shall give the owner of the boat another boat as compensation.

138. If a sailor wreck any one's ship, but saves it, he shall pay the half of its value in money.

139. If a man hire a sailor, he shall pay him six gur of corn per year.

140. If any one steal a water-wheel from the field, he shall pay five shekels in money to its owner.

141. If any one steal a shadduf (used to draw water from the river or canal) or a plow, he shall pay three shekels in money.

142. If any one hire a skilled artisan, he shall pay as wages . . . five gerahs, as wages of the potter five gerahs, of a tailor five gerahs, . . . of a ropemaker four gerahs, . . .

143. If any one hire a ferryboat, he shall pay three gerahs in money per day.

144. If he hire a freight-boat, he shall pay two and one-half gerahs per day.

Excerpts from *The Odyssey*
by Homer (c. 825 B.C.)

This is the opening section, in which Homer calls upon the Muse (the Muses were the goddesses of artistic inspiration) to tell through him the story of Odysseus. Translation by William Cowper.

Muse, make the man thy theme, for shrewdness famed
And genius versatile, who far and wide
A Wand'rer, after Ilium overthrown,
Discover'd various cities, and the mind
And manners learn'd of men, in lands remote.
He num'rous woes on Ocean toss'd, endured,
Anxious to save himself, and to conduct
His followers to their home; yet all his care
Preserved them not; they perish'd self-destroy'd
By their own fault; infatuate! who devoured
The oxen of the all-o'erseeing Sun,
And, punish'd for that crime, return'd no more.
Daughter divine of Jove, these things record,
As it may please thee, even in our ears.

Odysseus leaves the battle of Troy and heads home. Meanwhile, suitors try to win the heart of Odysseus' wife, Penelope, since they assume he will not return. Odysseus endures many dangers and adventures during the years it takes him to return home. He has conversations with gods who reveal to him the troubles he will face and how to overcome them. Odysseus also has encounters with many humans that test and delay him. Here Circe warns Odysseus of the dangerous Sirens and of Scylla and Charybdis, two huge rocks that will threaten to destroy his ship:

Thus far thy toils are finish'd. Now attend!
Mark well my words, of which the gods will sure
Themselves remind thee in the needful hour.
First shalt thou reach the Sirens; they the hearts
Enchant of all who on their coast arrive.
The wretch, who unforewarn'd approaching, hears
The Sirens' voice, his wife and little- ones
Ne'er fly to gratulate his glad return,
But him the Sirens sitting in the meads

Charm with mellifluous song, while all around
The bones accumulated lie of men
Now putrid, and the skins mould'ring away.
But, pass them thou, and, lest thy people hear
Those warblings, ere thou yet approach, fill all
Their ears with wax moulded between thy palms;
But as for thee—thou hear them if thou wilt.
Yet let thy people bind thee to the mast
Erect, encompassing thy feet and arms
With cordage well-secured to the mast-foot,
So shalt thou, raptur'd, hear the Sirens' song.
But if thou supplicate to be released,
Or give such order, then, with added cords
Let thy companions bind thee still the more.
When thus thy people shall have safely pass'd
The Sirens by, think not from me to learn
What course thou next shalt steer; two will occur;
Delib'rate chuse; I shall describe them both.
Here vaulted rocks impend, dash'd by the waves
Immense of Amphitrite azure-eyed;
The blessed gods those rocks, Erratic, call.
Birds cannot pass them safe; no, not the doves
Which his ambrosia bear to Father Jove,
But even of those doves the slipp'ry rock
Proves fatal still to one, for which the god
Supplies another, lest the number fail.
No ship, what ship soever there arrives,
Escapes them, but both mariners and planks
Whelm'd under billows of the Deep, or, caught
By fiery tempests, sudden disappear.

The phrase "a siren call" refers to an appeal that would lead to the destruction of the person who responds. We are warned by sirens on emergency vehicles. Scylla and Charybdis is probably the origin of the phrase "between a rock and a hard place."

Odysseus survives this and all the other tests he faces. He eventually makes it home,
wipes out the suitors, and settles down to home life once again.

Fables of Aesop (c. 550 B.C.)

Aesop was a slave from the island of Samos. He is associated with the use of fables for political purposes. Demetrius of Phaleron collected a large number of fables around 300 B.C. and called them fables of Aesop.

The Lion and the Mouse

Once when a Lion was asleep a little Mouse began running up and down upon him; this soon wakened the Lion, who placed his huge paw upon him, and opened his big jaws to swallow him.

"Pardon, O King," cried the little Mouse: "forgive me this time, I shall never forget it: who knows but what I may be able to do you a turn some of these days?"

The Lion was so tickled at the idea of the Mouse being able to help him, that he lifted up his paw and let him go. Some time after the Lion was caught in a trap, and the hunters, who desired to carry him alive to the King, tied him to a tree while they went in search of a wagon to carry him on. Just then the little Mouse happened to pass by, and seeing the sad plight in which the Lion was, went up to him and soon gnawed away the ropes that bound the King of the beasts.

"Was I not right?" said the little Mouse.

"Little friends may prove great friends."

The Fox and the Grapes

One hot summer's day a Fox was strolling through an orchard till he came to a bunch of Grapes just ripening on a vine which had been trained over a lofty branch. "Just the thing to quench my thirst," quoth he. Drawing back a few paces, he took a run and a jump, and just missed the bunch. Turning round again with a One, Two, Three, he jumped up, but with no greater success. Again and again he tried after the tempting morsel, but at last had to give it up, and walked away with his nose in the air, saying: "I am sure they are sour."

"It is easy to despise what you cannot get."

The Hart and the Hunter

The Hart was once drinking from a pool and admiring the noble figure he made there. "Ah," said he, "where can you see such noble horns as these, with such antlers! I wish I had legs more worthy to bear such a noble crown; it is a pity they are so slim and slight." At that moment a Hunter approached and sent an arrow whistling after him. Away bounded the Hart, and soon, by the aid of his nimble legs, was nearly out of sight of the Hunter; but not noticing where he was going, he passed under some trees with branches growing low down in which his antlers were caught, so that the Hunter had time to come up. "Alas! alas!" cried the Hart:

"We often despise what is most useful to us."

The Jay and the Peacock

A Jay venturing into a yard where Peacocks used to walk, found there a number of feathers which had fallen from the Peacocks when they were moulting. He tied them all to his tail and strutted down towards the Peacocks. When he came near them they soon discovered the cheat, and striding up to him pecked at him and plucked away his borrowed plumes. So the Jay could do no better than go back to the other Jays, who had watched his behaviour from a distance; but they were equally annoyed with him, and told him:

"It is not only fine feathers that make fine birds."

The Bald Man and the Fly

There was once a Bald Man who sat down after work on a hot summer's day. A Fly came up and kept buzzing about his bald pate, and stinging him from time to time. The Man aimed a blow at his little enemy, but – whack – his palm came on his head instead; again the Fly tormented him, but this time the Man was wiser and said:

"You will only injure yourself if you take notice of despicable enemies."

Androcles

A slave named Androcles once escaped from his master and fled to the forest. As he was wandering about there he came upon a Lion lying down moaning and groaning. At first he turned to flee, but finding that the Lion did not pursue him, he turned back and went up to him. As he came near, the Lion put out his paw, which was all swollen and bleeding, and Androcles found that a huge thorn had got into it, and was causing all the pain. He pulled out the thorn and bound up the paw of the Lion, who was soon able to rise and lick the hand of Androcles like a dog. Then the Lion took Androcles to his cave, and every day used to bring him meat from which to live. But shortly afterwards both Androcles and the Lion were captured, and the slave was sentenced to be thrown to the Lion, after the latter had been kept without food for several days. The Emperor and all his Court came to see the spectacle, and Androcles was led out into the middle of the arena. Soon the Lion was let loose from his den, and rushed bounding and roaring towards his victim. But as soon as he came near to Androcles he recognized his friend, and fawned upon him, and licked his hands like a friendly dog. The Emperor, surprised at this, summoned Androcles to him, who told him the whole story. Whereupon the slave was pardoned and freed, and the Lion let loose to his native forest.

"Gratitude is the sign of noble souls."

The Fox and the Mask

A fox had by some means got into the storeroom of a theatre. Suddenly he observed a face glaring down on him, and began to be very frightened; but looking more closely he found it was only a Mask such as actors use to put over their face.

"Ah," said the Fox, "you look very fine; it is a pity you have not got any brains."

"Outside show is a poor substitute for inner worth."

Excerpts from the *Analects*

(c. 500 B.C.)

The followers of the Chinese philosopher Confucius compiled his teachings, which later had a significant influence on Chinese culture and government.

Confucius said, "To learn and to practice what is learned time and again is pleasure, is it not? To have friends come from afar is happiness, is it not? To be unperturbed when not appreciated by others is gentlemanly, is it not?"

Yu Tzu (a disciple) said, "It is seldom that a man of filial piety (devotion to obeying his father) and brotherly love would be inclined to offend those above. There has not been a man inclined to cause disorder without the inclination to offend those above. The gentleman nourishes the roots. With the roots established, the way grows. Are filial piety and brotherly love not the roots of benevolence?"

Confucius

Confucius said, "Clever talk and a pretentious manner are seldom compatible with the benevolent."

Tseng Tzu (a disciple) said, "Each day I examine myself on three counts: whether or not I am loyal to those in whose behalf I act; whether or not I am trustworthy in my dealings with friends; whether or not I practice what is imparted."

Confucius said, "In leading a state of a thousand chariots (a large country), respect the office and be trustworthy; economize in the use of resources and love the people, and employ the people when it is timely.

Confucius said, "In the home, the young should behave with filial piety, and out in the world, with brotherly love. They should be prudent and trustworthy. They should love all people and be close to the benevolent. Having so done, their remaining strength should be used to learn literature."

Tzu Hsia (a disciple) said, "To revere virtue instead of beauty, to devote all strength to serving parents, to be willing to die in serving the lord (the emperor), to speak with trustworthiness in dealings with friends: even though it is said that such a one has not learned, I say he has."

Confucius said, "Without steadfastness, the gentleman would not command respect, and his learning would not be sound. Advocating loyalty and trustworthiness, he has no friend who is not his equal. He would not hesitate to correct his faults."

Tseng Tzu (a disciple) said, "To be prudent in mourning, and to remember those who have passed away before, is to enhance the virtue of the people."

Tzu Ch'in asked Tzu Kung (disciples), "To whichever state the Master (Confucius) travels, he always hears of its policies. Does he inquire or is he informed?" Tzu Kung replied, "The Master learns by being gentle, kind, courteous, modest, and deferential. The Master's inquiry is different from that of others."

Confucius said, "Note the aspirations of the man during his father's lifetime, and the conduct of the man after his father's death. If after three years he has not changed his father's way, this could be considered filial piety."

Yu Tzu (a disciple) said, "Harmony is the value of performing the rites (rules of etiquette, conduct, and moral obligations formalized during the Chou dynasty). Such was the beauty of the way of emperors past in matters great and small. Yet there are times when this is not acceptable. When there is harmony for harmony's sake, undisciplined by the rites, it is not acceptable."

Yu Tzu said, "When trustworthiness complements righteousness, words can be fulfilled. When courtesy complements the rites, shame and disgrace are kept afar. Thereby those closest are not lost and the honor of the ancestors is preserved."

Confucius said, "The gentleman does not seek to satiate himself in eating, does not seek ease in living, is quick in his dealings and prudent in speech, and keeps the company of men of principle that he may be rectified. He can be considered as devoted to learning."

Confucius said, "Do not be concerned about others not appreciating you. Be concerned about your not appreciating others."

Excerpts from the Twelve Tables of Roman Law (c. 451 B.C.)

The Twelve Tables of Law codified legal practices in the Roman Republic.

 If he (plaintiff) summon him (defendant) into court, he shall go. If he does not go, (plaintiff) shall call witnesses. Then only he shall take him by force. If he refuses or flees, he (plaintiff) shall lay hands on him. If disease or age is an impediment, he shall grant him a team (of oxen). He shall not spread with cushions the covered carriage if he does not wish to.

Whoever is in need of evidence, he shall go on every third day to call out loud before the doorway of the witness.

A dreadfully deformed child shall be killed.

Our ancestors saw fit that females, by reason of levity of disposition, shall remain in guardianship, even when they have attained their majority.

A spendthrift is forbidden to exercise administration over his own goods.

If any person has sung or composed against another person a song such as was causing slander or insult . . . he shall be clubbed to death.

If a person has maimed another's limb, let there be retaliation in kind, unless he agrees to make compensation with him.

Whoever is convicted of speaking false witness shall be flung from the Tarpeian Rock.

No person shall hold meetings in the City at night.

The penalty shall be capital punishment for a judge or arbiter legally appointed who has been found guilty of receiving a bribe for giving a decision.

Putting to death . . . of any man who has not been convicted, whosoever he might be, is forbidden.

Marriage shall not take place between a patrician and a plebeian.

Whatever the People have last ordained shall be held as binding by law.

The Funeral Oration of Pericles
(431 BC)

The Greek historian Thucydides preserved this eulogy for fallen Athenian soldiers offered by Pericles following one of the early battles of the Peloponnesian War. (Translated by Benjamin Jowett, 1881.)

Pericles

Most of those who have spoken here before me have commended the lawgiver who added this oration to our other funeral customs. It seemed to them a worthy thing that such an honor should be given at their burial to the dead who have fallen on the field of battle. But I should have preferred that, when men's deeds have been brave, they should be honored in deed only, and with such an honor as this public funeral, which you are now witnessing. Then the reputation of many would not have been imperiled on the eloquence or want of eloquence of one, and their virtues believed or not as he spoke well or ill. For it is difficult to say neither too little nor too much; and even moderation is apt not to give the impression of truthfulness.

The friend of the dead who knows the facts is likely to think that the words of the speaker fall short of his knowledge and of his wishes; another who is not so well informed, when he hears of anything which surpasses his own powers, will be envious and will suspect exaggeration. Mankind are tolerant of the praises of others so long as each hearer thinks that he can do as well or nearly as well himself, but, when the speaker rises above him, jealousy is aroused and he begins to be incredulous.

However, since our ancestors have set the seal of their approval upon the practice, I must obey, and to the utmost of my power shall endeavor to satisfy the wishes and beliefs of all who hear me.

I will speak first of our ancestors, for it is right and seemly that now, when we are lamenting the dead, a tribute should be paid to their memory. There has never been a time when they did not inhabit this land, which by their valor they will have handed down from generation to generation, and we have received from them a free state. But if they were worthy of praise, still more were our fathers, who added to their inheritance, and after many a struggle transmitted to us their sons this great empire. And we ourselves assembled here today, who are still most of us in the vigor of life, have carried the work of improvement further, and have richly endowed our city with all things, so that she is sufficient for herself both in peace and war.

Of the military exploits by which our various possessions were acquired, or of the energy with which we or our fathers drove back the tide of war, Hellenic or Barbarian, I will not speak; for the tale would be long and is familiar to you. But before I praise the dead, I should like to point out by what principles of action we rose to power, and under what institutions and through what manner of life our empire became great. For I conceive that such thoughts are not unsuited to the occasion, and that this numerous assembly of citizens and strangers may profitably listen to them.

Our form of government does not enter into rivalry with the institutions of others. Our government does not copy our neighbors', but is an example to them. It is true that we are called a democracy, for the administration is in the hands of the many and not of the few. But while there exists equal justice to all and alike in their private disputes, the claim of excellence is also recognized; and when a citizen is in any way distinguished, he is preferred to the public service, not as a matter of privilege, but as the reward of merit. Neither is poverty an obstacle, but a man may benefit his country whatever the obscurity of his condition.

There is no exclusiveness in our public life, and in our private business we are not suspicious of one another, nor angry with our neighbor if he does what he likes; we do not put on sour looks at him which, though harmless, are not pleasant. While we are thus unconstrained in our private business, a spirit of reverence pervades our public acts; we are prevented from doing wrong by respect for the authorities and for the laws, having a particular regard to those which are ordained for the protection of the injured as well as those unwritten laws which bring upon the transgressor of them the reprobation of the general sentiment.

And we have not forgotten to provide for our weary spirits many relaxations from toil; we have regular games and sacrifices throughout the year; our homes are beautiful and elegant; and the delight which we daily feel in all these things helps to banish sorrow. Because of the greatness of our city the fruits of the whole earth flow in upon us; so that we enjoy the goods of other countries as freely as our own.

Then, again, our military training is in many respects superior to that of our adversaries. Our city is thrown open to the world, and we never expel a foreigner and prevent him from seeing or learning anything of which the secret if revealed to an enemy might profit him. We rely not upon management or trickery, but upon our own hearts and hands. And in the matter of education, whereas they from early youth are always undergoing laborious exercises which are to make them brave, we live at ease, and yet are equally ready to face the perils which they face. And here is the proof: The Lacedaemonians come into Athenian territory not by themselves, but with their whole confederacy following; we go alone into a neighbor's country; and although our opponents are fighting for their homes and we on a foreign soil, we have seldom any difficulty in overcoming them.

Our enemies have never yet felt our united strength, the care of a navy divides our attention, and on land we are obliged to send our own citizens everywhere. But they, if they

Greek Warriors, c. 440 B.C.

meet and defeat a part of our army, are as proud as if they had routed us all, and when defeated they pretend to have been vanquished by us all.

If then we prefer to meet danger with a light heart but without laborious training, and with a courage which is gained by habit and not enforced by law, are we not greatly the better for it? Since we do not anticipate the pain, although, when the hour comes, we can be as brave as those who never allow themselves to rest; thus our city is equally admirable in peace and in war. For we are lovers of the beautiful in our tastes, and our strength lies, in our opinion, not in deliberation and discussion, but that knowledge which is gained by discussion preparatory to action. For we have a peculiar power of thinking before we act, and of acting, too, whereas other men are courageous from ignorance but hesitate upon reflection. And they are surely to be esteemed the bravest spirits who, having the clearest sense both of the pains and pleasures of life, do not on that account shrink from danger.

In doing good, again, we are unlike others; we make our friends by conferring, not by receiving favors. Now he who confers a favor is the firmer friend, because he would rather by kindness keep alive the memory of an obligation; but the recipient is colder in his feelings, because he knows that in requiting another's generosity he will not be winning gratitude but only paying a debt. We alone do good to our neighbors not upon a calculation of interest, but in the confidence of freedom and in a frank and fearless spirit. To sum up: I say that Athens is the school of Hellas, and that the individual Athenian in his own person seems to have the power of adapting himself to the most varied forms of action with the utmost versatility and grace. This is no passing and idle word, but truth and fact; and the assertion is verified by the position to which these qualities have raised the state. For in the hour of trial Athens alone among her contemporaries is superior to the report of her. No enemy who comes against her is indignant at the reverses which he sustains at the hands of such a city; no subject complains that his masters are unworthy of him. And we shall assuredly not be without witnesses; there are mighty monuments of our power which will make us the wonder of this and of succeeding ages; we shall not need the praises of Homer or of any other panegyrist whose poetry may please for the moment, although his representation of the facts will not bear the light of day. For we have compelled every land and every sea to open a path for our valor, and have everywhere planted eternal memorials of our friendship and of our enmity. Such is the city for whose sake these men nobly fought and died; they could not bear the thought that she might be taken from them; and every one of us who survive should gladly toil on her behalf.

I have dwelt upon the greatness of Athens because I want to show you that we are contending for a higher prize than those who enjoy none of these privileges, and to establish by manifest proof the merit of these men whom I am now commemorating. Their loftiest praise has been already spoken. For in magnifying the city I have magnified them, and men like them whose virtues made her glorious. And of how few Hellenes can it be said as of them, that their deeds when weighed in the balance have been found equal to their fame! Methinks that a death such as theirs has been the true measure of a man's worth; it may be the first revelation of his virtues, but is at any rate their final seal. For even those who come short in other ways may justly plead the valor with which they have fought for their country; they have blotted out the evil with the good, and have benefited the state more by their public services than they have injured her by their private actions.

None of these men were enervated by wealth or hesitated to resign the pleasures of life; none of them put off the evil day in the hope, natural to poverty, that a man, though poor, may one day become rich. But, deeming that the punishment of their enemies was sweeter than any of these things, and that they could fall in no nobler cause, they determined at the hazard of their lives to be honorably avenged, and to leave the rest. They resigned to hope their unknown chance of happiness; but in the face of death they resolved to rely upon themselves alone. And when the moment came they were minded to resist and suffer, rather than to fly and save their lives; they ran away from the word of dishonor, but on the battlefield their feet stood fast, and in an instant, at the height of their fortune, they passed away from the scene, not of their fear, but of their glory.

Such was the end of these men; they were worthy of Athens, and the living need not desire to have a more heroic spirit, although they may pray for a less fatal issue. The value of such a spirit is not to be expressed in words. Any one can discourse to you for ever about the advantages of a brave defense, which you know already. But instead of listening to him I would have you day by day fix your eyes upon the greatness of Athens, until you become filled with the love of her; and when you are impressed by the spectacle of her glory, reflect that this empire has been acquired by men who knew their duty and had the courage to do it, who in the hour of conflict had the fear of dishonor always present to them, and who, if ever they failed in an enterprise, would not allow their virtues to be lost to their country, but freely gave their lives to her as the fairest offering which they could present at her feast. The sacrifice which they collectively made was individually repaid to them; for they received again each one for himself a praise which grows not old, and the noblest of all tombs – I speak not of that in which their remains are laid, but of that in which their glory survives, and is proclaimed always and on every fitting occasion both in word and deed.

For the whole earth is the tomb of famous men; not only are they commemorated by columns and inscriptions in their own country, but in foreign lands there dwells also an unwritten memorial of them, graven not on stone but in the hearts of men. Make them your examples, and, esteeming courage to be freedom and freedom to be happiness, do not weigh too nicely the perils of war. The unfortunate who has no hope of a change for the better has less reason to throw away his life than the prosperous who, if he survive, is always liable to a change for the worse, and to whom any accidental fall makes the most serious difference. To a man of spirit, cowardice and disaster coming together are far more bitter than death striking him unperceived at a time when he is full of courage and animated by the general hope.

Wherefore I do not now pity the parents of the dead who stand here; I would rather comfort them. You know that your dead have passed away amid manifold vicissitudes; and that they may be deemed fortunate who have gained their utmost honor, whether an honorable death like theirs, or an honorable sorrow like yours, and whose share of happiness has been so ordered that the term of their happiness is likewise the term of their life. I know how hard it is to make you feel this, when the good fortune of others will too often remind you of the gladness which once lightened your hearts. And sorrow is felt at the want of those blessings, not which a man never knew, but which were a part of his life before they were taken from him. Some of you are of an age at which they may hope to have other children, and they ought to bear their sorrow better; not only will the children who may hereafter be born make them forget their own lost ones, but the city will be doubly a gainer. She will not be left desolate, and she will be safer. For a man's counsel cannot have equal weight or worth, when he alone has no children to risk in the general danger. To those of you who have passed their prime, I say: "Congratulate yourselves that you have been happy during the greater part of your days; remember that your life of sorrow will not last long, and be comforted by the glory of those who are gone." For the love of honor alone is ever young, and not riches, as some say, but honor is the delight of men when they are old and useless.

To you who are the sons and brothers of the departed, I see that the struggle to emulate them will be an arduous one. For all men praise the dead, and, however preeminent your virtue may be, I do not say even to approach them, and avoid living their rivals and detractors, but when a man is out of the way, the honor and goodwill which he receives is unalloyed. And, if I am to speak of womanly virtues to those of you who will henceforth be widows, let me sum them up in one short admonition: To a woman not to show more weakness than is natural to her sex is a great glory, and not to be talked about for good or for evil among men.

I have paid the required tribute, in obedience to the law, making use of such fitting words as I had. The tribute of deeds has been paid in part; for the dead have them in deeds, and it remains only that their children should be maintained at the public charge until they are grown up: this is the solid prize with which, as with a garland, Athens crowns her sons living and dead, after a struggle like theirs. For where the rewards of virtue are greatest, there the noblest citizens are enlisted in the service of the state. And now, when you have duly lamented every one his own dead, you may depart.

The Hippocratic Oath

(c. 400 B.C.)

The Hippocratic Oath laid down high standards for medical practice, though its direct association with Hippocrates is uncertain. Doctors have used it as a basis of medical practice for centuries. A modern version (that does not mention abortion and other issues) was written in 1964 and is used in many places today.

The Original Hippocratic Oath

I swear by Apollo the physician, by Aesculapius, and Health, and All-heal, and all the gods and goddesses, that according to my ability and my judgment, I will keep this Oath and this stipulation— to reckon him who taught me this Art equally dear to me as my parents, to share my substance with him, and relieve his necessities if required to look upon his offspring in the same footing as my own brothers, and to teach them this Art, if they wish to learn it, without fee or stipulation; and that by precept, lecture, and every mode of instruction, I will impart a knowledge of the Art to my own sons, and those of my teachers, and to disciples bound by a stipulation and oath according to the law of medicine, but to none others.

I will follow that system or regimen which, according to my ability and judgment, I consider for the benefit of my patients, and abstain from whatever is deleterious and mischievous.

I will give no deadly medicine to any one if asked, nor suggest any such counsel; and in like manner I will not give to a woman a pessary to produce abortion.

With purity and with holiness I will pass my life and practice my Art. I will not cut persons laboring under the stone, but will leave this to be done by men who are practitioners of this work. Into whatever houses I enter, I will go into them for the benefit of the sick and will abstain from every voluntary act of mischief and corruption; and, further from the seduction of females and males, of freemen and slaves.

Whatever, in connection with my professional service, or not in connection with it, I see or hear, in the life of men, which ought not to be spoken of abroad, I will not divulge, as reckoning that all such should be kept secret.

While I continue to keep this Oath unviolated, may it be granted to me to enjoy life and practice of the Art, respected by all men, in all times. But should I trespass and violate this Oath, may the reverse be my lot.

Hippocratic Oath – Modern Version

I swear to fulfill, to the best of my ability and judgment, this covenant:

I will respect the hard-won scientific gains of those physicians in whose steps I walk, and gladly share such knowledge as is mine with those who are to follow.

I will apply, for the benefit of the sick, all measures which are required, avoiding those twin traps of overtreatment and therapeutic nihilism.

I will remember that there is art to medicine as well as science, and that warmth, sympathy, and understanding may outweigh the surgeon's knife or the chemist's drug.

I will not be ashamed to say "I know not," nor will I fail to call in my colleagues when the skills of another are needed for a patient's recovery.

I will respect the privacy of my patients, for their problems are not disclosed to me that the world may know. Most especially must I tread with care in matters of life and death. If it is given me to save a life, all thanks. But it may also be within my power to take a life; this awesome responsibility must be faced with great humbleness and awareness of my own frailty. Above all, I must not play at God.

I will remember that I do not treat a fever chart, a cancerous growth, but a sick human being, whose illness may affect the person's family and economic stability. My responsibility includes these related problems, if I am to care adequately for the sick.

I will prevent disease whenever I can, for prevention is preferable to cure.

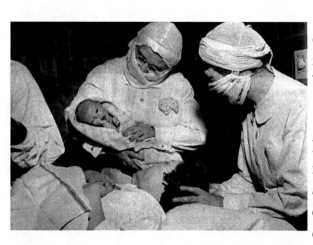

I will remember that I remain a member of society, with special obligations to all my fellow human beings, those sound of mind and body as well as the infirm.

If I do not violate this oath, may I enjoy life and art, respected while I live and remembered with affection thereafter. May I always act so as to preserve the finest traditions of my calling and may I long experience the joy of healing those who seek my help.

Excerpt from *Cyropaedia*
by Xenophon (c. 400 B.C.)

*Xenophon was a Greek writer who lived about a century after Cyrus. His biography of Cyrus
is not necessarily reliable historically, but it provides an interesting interpretation of his life.
(Translated by Henry Graham Dakyns. Revised by F. M. Stawell.)*

[C.7] Thus the years passed on, and Cyrus was now in a ripe old age, and he journeyed to Persia for the seventh time in his reign. His father and mother were long since dead in the course of nature, and Cyrus offered sacrifice according to the law, and led the sacred dance of his Persians after the manner of his forefathers, and gave gifts to every man according to his wont.

[2] But one night, as he lay asleep in the royal palace, he dreamt a dream. It seemed to him that some one met him, greater than a man, and said to him, "Set your house in order, Cyrus: the time has come, and you are going to the gods."

With that Cyrus awoke out of sleep, and he all but seemed to know that the end of his life was at hand. [3] Straightway he took victims and offered sacrifice to Zeus, the god of his fathers, and to the Sun, and all the other gods, on the high places where the Persians sacrifice, and then he made this prayer:

"Zeus, god of my fathers, and thou, O Sun, and all ye gods, accept this sacrifice, my offering for many a noble enterprise, and suffer me to thank you for the grace ye have shown me, telling me all my life, by victims and by signs from heaven, by birds and by the voices of men, what things I ought to do and what I ought to refrain from doing. Deep is my thankfulness that I was able to recognise your care, and never lifted up my heart too high even in my prosperity. I beseech you now to bless my children also, and my wife, and my friends, and my fatherland; and for myself, may my death be as my life has been."

[4] Then Cyrus went home again and lay down on his bed, for he longed to rest. And when the hour was come, his attendants came to him and bade him take his bath. But he said he would rather rest. And others came afterwards, at the usual time, to set the meal before him; but he could not bring himself to take food: he seemed only to thirst, and drank readily. [5] It was the same the second day, and the third, and then he called his sons to his side—it chanced they had followed him to Persia—and he summoned his friends also and the chief magistrates of the land, and when they were all met, he began:

Persian King, Official, and Attendant

[6] "My sons, and friends of mine, the end of my life is at hand: I know it by many signs. And when I am dead, you must show by word and deed that you think of me as happy. When I was a child, I had all the joys and triumphs of a child, and I reaped the treasures of youth as I grew up, and all the glories of a man when I came to man's estate. And as the years passed, I seemed to find my powers grow with them, so that I never felt my old age weaker than my youth, nor can I think of anything I attempted or desired wherein I failed. [7] Moreover, I have seen my friends made happy by my means, and my enemies crushed beneath my hand. This my fatherland, which was once of no account in Asia, I leave at the height of power, and of all that I won I think I have lost nothing. Throughout my whole life I have fared as I prayed to fare, and the dread that was ever with me lest in days to come I might see or hear or suffer evil, this dread would never let me think too highly of myself, or rejoice as a fool rejoices. [8] And if I die now, I leave my sons behind me, the sons the gods have given me; and I leave my fatherland in happiness, and my friends. Surely I may hope that men will count me blessed and cherish my memory.

[9] And now I must leave instructions about my kingdom, that there may be no dispute among you after my death. Sons of mine, I love you both alike, but I choose the elder-born, the one whose experience of life is the greater, to be the leader in council and the guide in action. [10] Thus was I trained myself, in the fatherland that is yours and mine, to yield to my elders, my brothers or my fellow-citizens, in the street, or in the place of meeting, or in the assembly for debate. And thus have I trained both of you, to honour your elders and be honoured by those who are younger than yourselves. These are the principles that I leave with you, sanctioned by time, ingrained in our customs, embodied in our laws. [11] The sovereignty is yours, Cambyses; the gods have given it to you, and I also, as far as in me lies; and to you, Tanaoxares, I give the satrapy over the Medes and the Armenians and the Cadousians, these three; and though I leave your elder brother a larger empire and the name of king, your inheritance will bring you, I believe, more perfect happiness than his. [12] I ask myself what human joy will be lacking to you: all things which gladden the hearts of men will be yours—but the craving for what is out of reach, the load of cares, the restless passion to rival my achievements, the plots and counterplots, they will follow him who wears the crown, and they are things, be well assured, that leave little leisure for happiness. [13] And you, Cambyses, you know of yourself, without words from me, that your kingdom is not guarded by this golden sceptre, but by faithful friends; their loyalty is your true staff, a sceptre which shall not fail. But never think that loyal hearts grow up by nature as the grass grows in the field: if that were so, the same men would be loyal to all alike, even as all natural objects are the same to all mankind. No, every leader must win his own followers for himself, and the way to win them is not by violence but by loving-kindness."

Excerpt from *The Republic*
by Plato (c. 375 B.C.)

In Book 7 of The Republic, "On Shadows and Realities in Education," Plato uses an allegory to show how we learn, how we perceive reality, and what we do when confronted with new information. Socrates is portrayed as the teacher, speaking in first person, and the pupil is Glaucon. (Translated by Benjamin Jowett, 1901.)

And now, I said, let me show in a figure how far our nature is enlightened or unenlightened: Behold! human beings living in an underground den, which has a mouth open toward the light and reaching all along the den; here they have been from their childhood, and have their legs and necks chained so that they cannot move, and can only see before them, being prevented by the chains from turning round their heads. Above and behind them a fire is blazing at a distance, and between the fire and the prisoners there is a raised way; and you will see, if you look, a low wall built along the way, like the screen which marionette-players have in front of them, over which they show the puppets.

Plato

I see.

And do you see, I said, men passing along the wall carrying all sorts of vessels, and statues and figures of animals made of wood and stone and various materials, which appear over the wall? Some of them are talking, others silent.

You have shown me a strange image, and they are strange prisoners.

Like ourselves, I replied; and they see only their own shadows, or the shadows of one another, which the fire throws on the opposite wall of the cave?

True, he said; how could they see anything but the shadows if they were never allowed to move their heads?

And of the objects which are being carried in like manner they would only see the shadows?

Yes, he said.

Socrates

And if they were able to converse with one another, would they not suppose that they were naming what was actually before them?

Very true.

And suppose further that the prison had an echo which came from the other side, would they not be sure to fancy when one of the passers-by spoke that the voice which they heard came from the passing shadow?

No question, he replied.

To them, I said, the truth would be literally nothing but the shadows of the images.

That is certain.

And now look again, and see what will naturally follow if the prisoners are released and disabused of their error. At first, when any of them is liberated and compelled suddenly to stand up and turn his neck round and walk and look toward the light, he will suffer sharp pains; the glare will distress him, and he will be unable to see the realities of which in his former state he had seen the shadows; and then conceive someone saying to him, that what he saw before was an illusion, but that now, when he is approaching nearer to being and his eye is turned toward more real existence, he has a clearer vision – what will be his reply? And you may further imagine that his instructor is pointing to the objects as they pass and requiring him to name them – will he not be perplexed? Will he not fancy that the shadows which he formerly saw are truer than the objects which are now shown to him?

Far truer.

And if he is compelled to look straight at the light, will he not have a pain in his eyes which will make him turn away to take refuge in the objects of vision which he can see, and which he will conceive to be in reality clearer than the things which are now being shown to him?

True, he said.

And suppose once more, that he is reluctantly dragged up a steep and rugged ascent, and held fast until he is forced into the presence of the sun himself, is he not likely to be pained and irritated? When he approaches the light his eyes will be dazzled, and he will not be able to see anything at all of what are now called realities.

Not all in a moment, he said.

He will require to grow accustomed to the sight of the upper world. And first he will see the shadows best, next the reflections of men and other objects in the water, and then the objects themselves; then he will gaze upon the light of the moon and the stars and the spangled heaven; and he will see the sky and the stars by night better than the sun or the light of the sun by day?

Certainly.

Last of all he will be able to see the sun, and not mere reflections of him in the water, but he will see him in his own proper place, and not in another; and he will contemplate him as he is.

Certainly.

He will then proceed to argue that this is he who gives the season and the years, and is the guardian of all that is in the visible world, and in a certain way the cause of all things which he and his fellows have been accustomed to behold?

Clearly, he said, he would first see the sun and then reason about him.

And when he remembered his old habitation, and the wisdom of the den and his fellow-prisoners, do you not suppose that he would felicitate himself on the change, and pity him?

Certainly, he would. . . .

Letters Between Pliny the Younger and Emperor Trajan (c. 112)

Pliny the Younger was Governor of Bithynia in Asia Minor. The information about Christians he reports in the letter might not be reliable. Most of it comes from a skeptical governor, people who had renounced Christ, and two women who led in some kind of service, which would have been highly unlikely in a group closely following the apostles' teachings.

Pliny's Letter to Trajan

It is my invariable rule, Sir, to refer to you in all matters where I feel doubtful; for who is more capable of removing my scruples, or informing my ignorance? Having never been present at any trials concerning those who profess Christianity, I am unacquainted not only with the nature of their crimes, or the measure of their punishment, but how far it is proper to enter into an examination concerning them. Whether, therefore, any difference is usually made with respect to ages, or no distinction is to be observed between the young and the adult; whether repentance entitles them to a pardon, or, if a man has been once a Christian, it avails nothing to desist from his error; whether the very profession of Christianity, unattended with any criminal act, or only the crimes themselves inherent in the profession are punishable; on all these points I am in great doubt.

In the meanwhile, the method I have observed towards those who have been brought before me as Christians is this: I asked them whether they were Christians; if they admitted it, I repeated the question twice, and threatened them with punishment; if they persisted, I ordered them to be at once punished: for I was persuaded, whatever the nature of their opinions might be, a contumacious and inflexible obstinacy certainly deserved correction.

There were others also brought before me possessed with the same infatuation, but being Roman citizens, I directed them to be sent to Rome. But this crime spreading (as is usually the case) while it was actually under prosecution, several instances of the same nature occurred. An anonymous information was laid before me containing a charge against several persons, who upon examination denied they were Christians, or had ever been so. They repeated after me an invocation to the gods, and offered religious rites with wine and incense before your statue (which for that purpose I had ordered to be brought, together with those of the gods), and even reviled the name of Christ: whereas there is no forcing, it is said, those who are really Christians into any of these compliances: I thought it proper, therefore, to discharge them.

Some among those who were accused by a witness in person at first confessed themselves Christians, but immediately after denied it; the rest owned indeed that they had been of that number formerly, but had now (some above three, others more, and a few above twenty years ago) renounced that error. They all worshiped your statue and the images of the gods, uttering imprecations at the same time against the name of Christ. They affirmed the whole of their guilt, or their error, was, that they met on a stated day before it was light, and addressed a form of prayer to Christ, as to a divinity, binding themselves by a solemn oath, not for the purposes of any wicked design, but never to commit any fraud, theft, or adultery, never to falsify their word, nor deny a trust when they should be called upon to deliver it up; after which it was their custom to separate, and then reassemble, to eat in common a harmless meal. From this custom, however, they desisted after the publication of my edict, by which, according to your commands, I forbade the meeting of any assemblies.

After receiving this account, I judged it so much the more necessary to endeavour to extort the real truth, by putting two female slaves to the torture, who were said to officiate in their religious rites: but all I could discover was evidence of an absurd and extravagant superstition. I deemed it expedient, therefore, to adjourn all further proceedings, in order to consult you. For it appears to be a matter highly deserving your consideration, more especially as great numbers must be involved in the danger of these prosecutions, which have already extended, and are still likely to extend, to persons of all ranks and ages, and even of both sexes. In fact, this contagious superstition is not confined to the cities only, but has spread its infection among the neighbouring villages and country.

Nevertheless, it still seems possible to restrain its progress. The temples, at least, which were once almost deserted, begin now to be frequented; and the sacred rites, after a long intermission, are again revived; while there is a general demand for the victims, which till lately found very few purchasers. From all this it is easy to conjecture what numbers might be reclaimed if a general pardon were granted to those who shall repent of their error.

Trajan's Reply to Pliny

You have adopted the right course, my dearest Secundus, in investigating the charges against the Christians who were brought before you. It is not possible to lay down any general rule for all such cases. Do not go out of your way to look for them. If indeed they should be brought before you, and the crime is proved, they must be punished; with the restriction, however, that where the party denies he is a Christian, and shall make it evident that he is not, by invoking our gods, let him (notwithstanding any former suspicion) be pardoned upon his repentance. Anonymous informations ought not to be received in any sort of prosecution. It is introducing a very dangerous precedent, and is quite foreign to the spirit of our age.

Excerpt from the Letter to Diognetus
(date uncertain, perhaps early 100s)

This anonymous apologetic letter has not yet been dated with certainty, but many scholars place it early in the second century. The recipient, Diognetus, has also been the subject of much debate. The section below is a brilliant summary of the way of Christians.

For the Christians are distinguished from other men neither by country, nor language, nor the customs which they observe. For they neither inhabit cities of their own, nor employ a peculiar form of speech, nor lead a life which is marked out by any singularity. The course of conduct which they follow has not been devised by any speculation or deliberation of inquisitive men; nor do they, like some, proclaim themselves the advocates of any merely human doctrines. But, inhabiting Greek as well as barbarian cities, according as the lot of each of them has determined, and following the customs of the natives in respect to clothing, food, and the rest of their ordinary conduct, they display to us their wonderful and confessedly striking method of life. They dwell in their own countries, but simply as sojourners. As citizens, they share in all things with others, and yet endure all things as if foreigners. Every foreign land is to them as their native country, and every land of their birth as a land of strangers. They marry, as do all [others]; they beget children; but they do not destroy their offspring. They have a common table, but not a common bed. They are in the flesh, but they do not live after the flesh. They pass their days on earth, but they are citizens of heaven. They obey the prescribed laws, and at the same time surpass the laws by their lives. They love all men, and are persecuted by all. They are unknown and condemned; they are put to death, and restored to life. They are poor, yet make many rich; they are in lack of all things, and yet abound in all; they are dishonoured, and yet in their very dishonour are glorified. They are evil spoken of, and yet are justified; they are reviled, and bless; they are insulted, and repay the insult with honour; they do good, yet are punished as evil-doers. When punished, they rejoice as if quickened into life; they are assailed by the Jews as foreigners, and are persecuted by the Greeks; yet those who hate them are unable to assign any reason for their hatred.

Shepherd of Tender Youth
by Clement of Alexandria (c. 200)

Probably the oldest hymn whose author is known is this one
attributed to Titus Flavius Clemens, known as Clement of Alexandria.

Shepherd of tender youth, guiding in love and truth
Through devious ways; Christ our triumphant King,
We come Thy Name to sing and here our children bring
To join Thy praise.

Thou art our holy Lord, O all subduing Word,
Healer of strife. Thou didst Thyself abase
That from sin's deep disgrace Thou mightest save our race
And give us life.

Thou art the great High Priest; Thou hast prepared the feast
Of holy love; and in our mortal pain,
None calls on Thee in vain; Help Thou dost not disdain,
Help from above.

Ever be Thou our guide, our shepherd and our pride,
Our staff and song; Jesus, Thou Christ of God,
By Thine enduring Word lead us where Thou hast trod,
Make our faith strong.

So now, and till we die, sound we Thy praises high
And joyful sing; infants and the glad throng
Who to Thy church belong, unite to swell the song
To Christ, our King.

Clement of Alexandria

The Edict of Milan

(313)

The Emperor Galerius had proposed toleration for Christians in 311, but this statement by Constantine and his co-emperor Licinius Augustus gave special recognition to Christianity.

CONSTANTINVS AVG

When I, Constantine Augustus, as well as I, Licinius Augustus, fortunately met near Mediolanurn (Milan), and were considering everything that pertained to the public welfare and security, we thought, among other things which we saw would be for the good of many, those regulations pertaining to the reverence of the Divinity ought certainly to be made first, so that we might grant to the Christians and others full authority to observe that religion which each preferred; whence any Divinity whatsoever in the seat of the heavens may be propitious and kindly disposed to us and all who are placed under our rule. And thus by this wholesome counsel and most upright provision we thought to arrange that no one whatsoever should be denied the opportunity to give his heart to the observance of the Christian religion, of that religion which he should think best for himself, so that the Supreme Deity, to whose worship we freely yield our hearts, may show in all things His usual favor and benevolence. Therefore, your Worship should know that it has pleased us to remove all conditions whatsoever, which were in the rescripts formerly given to you officially, concerning the Christians and now any one of these who wishes to observe Christian religion may do so freely and openly, without molestation. We thought it fit to commend these things most fully to your care that you may know that we have given to those Christians free and unrestricted opportunity of religious worship. When you see that this has been granted to them by us, your Worship will know that we have also conceded to other religions the right of open and free observance of their worship for the sake of the peace of our times, that each one may have the free opportunity to worship as he pleases; this regulation is made that we may not seem to detract from any dignity or any religion.

Moreover, in the case of the Christians especially we esteemed it best to order that if it happens anyone heretofore has bought from our treasury from anyone whatsoever, those places where they were previously accustomed to assemble, concerning which a certain decree had been made and a letter sent to you officially, the same shall be restored to the Christians without payment or any claim of recompense and without any kind of fraud or deception. Those, moreover, who have obtained the same by gift, are likewise to return them at once to the Christians. Besides, both those who have purchased and those who have secured them by gift, are to appeal to the vicar if they seek any recompense from our bounty, that they may be cared for through our clemency. All this property ought to be delivered at once to the community of the Christians through your intercession, and without delay. And since these Christians are known to have possessed not only those places in which they were accustomed to assemble, but also other property, namely the churches, belonging to them as a corporation and not as individuals, all these things which we have included under the above law, you will order to be restored, without any hesitation or controversy at all, to these Christians, that is to say to the corporations and their conventicles: providing, of course, that the above arrangements be followed so that those who return the same without payment, as we have said, may hope for an indemnity from our bounty. In all these circumstances you ought to tender your most efficacious intervention to the community of the Christians, that our command may be carried into effect as quickly as possible, whereby, moreover, through our clemency, public order may be secured. Let this be done so that, as we have said above, Divine favor towards us, which, under the most important circumstances we have already experienced, may, for all time, preserve and prosper our successes together with the good of the state. Moreover, in order that the statement of this decree of our good will may come to the notice of all, this rescript, published by your decree, shall be announced everywhere and brought to the knowledge of all, so that the decree of this, our benevolence, cannot be concealed.

Fourth-century Christian Commoners

The Dawn Is Sprinkling in the East
by Ambrose of Milan (c. 300s)

This hymn, attributed to Ambrose of Milan, was translated
from Latin to English in 1849 by Edward Casswall.

The dawn is sprinkling in the east
Its golden shower, as day flows in;
Fast mount the pointed shafts of light:
Farewell to darkness and to sin!

Away, ye midnight phantoms all!
Away, despondence and despair!
Whatever guilt the night has brought
Now let it vanish into air.

So, Lord, when that last morning breaks,
Looking to which we sigh and pray,
O may it to Thy minstrels prove
The dawning of a better day.

To God the Father glory be,
And to His sole begotten Son;
Glory, O Holy Ghost, to Thee
While everlasting ages run.

Ambrose of Milan

Lord Jesus, Think On Me
by Synesius of Cyrene (c. 430)

Translated by Allen W. Catfield and published in 1876
in Songs and Hymns of Earliest Greek Christian Poets

Lord Jesus, think on me
And purge away my sin;
From earthborn passions set me free
And make me pure within.

Lord Jesus, think on me,
With many a care oppressed;
Let me Thy loving servant be
And taste Thy promised rest.

Lord Jesus, think on me
Amid the battle's strife;
In all my pain and misery
Be Thou my Health and Life.

Lord Jesus, think on me
Nor let me go astray;
Through darkness and perplexity
Point Thou the heavenly way.

Lord Jesus, think on me
When floods the tempest high;
When on doth rush the enemy,
O Savior, be Thou nigh!

Lord Jesus, think on me
That, when the flood is past,
I may th'eternal brightness see
And share Thy joy at last.

Lord Jesus, think on me
That I may sing above
To Father, Spirit, and to Thee
The strains of praise and love.

Hymns by Columba (500s)

Columba was born on December 7, 521 in County Donegal, Ireland. He became a priest and in 563 went to Scotland, where he served as a missionary to the northern Picts. He is said to have been one of the first to see the "Loch Ness Monster."

O God, Thou Art the Father

O God, Thou art the Father
Of all that have believed;
From whom all hosts of angels
Have life and power received.
O God, thou art the Maker
Of all created things,
The righteous Judge of judges,
Th'almighty King of kings.

High in the heavenly Zion
Thou reignest God adored;
And in the coming glory
Thou shalt be sovereign Lord.
Beyond our ken Thou shinest,
The everlasting Light;
Ineffable in loving,
Unthinkable in might.

Thou to the meek and lowly
Thy secrets dost unfold;
O God, Thou doest all things,
All things both new and old.
I walk secure and blessèd
In every clime or coast,
In name of God the Father,
And Son, and Holy Ghost.

Christ Is the World's Redeemer

Christ is the world's Redeemer,
The lover of the pure,
The Fount of heavenly wisdom,
Our trust and hope secure;
The Armor of His soldiers,
The Lord of earth and sky;
Our Health while we are living,
Our Life when we shall die.

All glory to the Father,
The unbegotten One;
All honor be to Jesus,
His sole begotten Son;
And to the Holy Spirit—
The perfect Trinity.
Let all the worlds give answer,
"Amen—so let it be."

Christian, Dost Thou See Them?
by Andrew of Crete (c. 600s)

Andrew was born in Damascus, Syria and became a monk at Mar Saba, Israel.
Later, he served in Jerusalem, Constantinople, and finally, Crete.
He ran an orphanage and cared for the elderly. This hymn was translated from the Greek
by John M. Neale and published in 1869 in Hymns of the Eastern Church.

hristian, dost thou see them on the holy ground,
How the powers of darkness rage thy steps around?
Christian, up and smite them, counting gain but loss,
In the strength that cometh by the holy cross.
Christian, dost thou feel them, how they work within,
Striving, tempting, luring, goading into sin?
Christian, never tremble; never be downcast;
Gird thee for the battle, watch and pray and fast.
Christian, dost thou hear them, how they speak thee fair?
Always fast and vigil? Always watch and prayer?
Christian, answer boldly: While I breathe I pray!
Peace shall follow battle, night shall end in day.
Well I know thy trouble, O my servant true;
Thou art very weary, I was weary, too;
But that toil shall make thee some day all Mine own,
At the end of sorrow shall be near my throne.

Excerpt from *Historia Ecclesiastica Gentis Anglorum (The History of the Primitive Church of England)* by Bede (c. 731)

Bede's history provides a description of the history of England from the Roman invasion to about 600 AD. His purpose was to emphasize the arrival and spread of Christianity in England.
(Translated by William Hurst, 1814)

Book One, Chapter One

Of the situation of Britain and of Ireland, and of their ancient Inhabitants.

Britain, an island in the Atlantic Ocean, was formerly called Albion, and lies opposite to the principal parts of the continent of Europe, at some distance from Germany, Gaul and Spain. It is 800 miles in length, and only about 200 miles in its main breadth, But if you take into the account every promontory and tract of land projecting into the sea, it will be found to be about 4,875 miles in circumference.

Bede

The nearest country to it towards the South is the province of the Morini, [now called the Department of the Straits of Calais,] and the passage by sea to Gessoriacum [which is the town of Calais] is about seven leagues or 21 miles. On the north side, the Isles called Orcades [Orkneys] are not far distant from it. The island is very fertile in corn, fruit, and trees, and abounds in pasture for cattle. It also produces vines in some places, and is plentifully supplied with land and water fowls, of different kinds; and is remarkable for brooks and rivers well stored with fish; particularly with salmon and eels. The surrounding sea affords seals, dolphins, and whales; besides many sorts of shell-fish; among which are oysters, and in them are often found excellent pearls of all colours, viz. red, pale, violet, and green; but they are mostly of a white colour. There is also a kind of shell-fish, of which the scarlet dye is made; which beautiful colour never fades with the heat of the sun, or from the effects of rain, but the older it grows the more bright and brilliant it becomes.

Many springs are found in different parts of the island, the waters of some of which are of such a nature as to yield a great quantity of salt. There are also several others of mineral waters, over which convenient structures have been raised to accommodate such persons as wish to take the benefit of the hot baths. [The Romans built a bath over a hot spring in southwestern England. The town is called Bath, and thousands of gallons of hot mineral water flow daily from the spring to this day.—RN] For water, as St. Basil observes

[Hexaemeron, 4.6], receives a healing quality when it runs over certain metals, and sometimes becomes very hot.

The metals which are generally found here are lead, iron, copper, and silver. There is also a sort of stone, which is commonly called Jeat, or Geat, and is black and sparkling. It glitters when near the fire, and being heated, is said to have the property of driving away serpents. If it be warmed with rubbing, it attracts things to it, like amber.

The island was formerly embellished with 28 well-built cities, besides innumerable castles, all of which were also strongly fortified with walls, towers, gates, and bulwarks. As it is situated almost under the North Pole, the days are so long in summer that even at midnight in the northern parts a kind of twilight continues. But, in the winter, the nights for the same reason are very long, the darkness continuing for 17 or 18 hours; whereas in Armenia, Macedon, Italy, and other countries, in the same latitude, the longest day or night extends but to 15 hours, and the shortest to 9.

There are at present five different languages spoken in this island, viz. the British, the English, the Scottish, and those of the Picts and of the Latins, according to the different nations who at various periods have taken possession of it, and who all profess the same Christian faith, and the sublime morality of the gospel. The Latin language in particular, on account of their continual application to the study of the Scriptures, is become common everywhere.

At first, this country had no other inhabitants but the Britons, from whom it derived its name, who sailing from Brittany, [now called the Department of Finisterre in France,] successfully invaded the southern coasts; and, when they had conquered the greatest part of it, it happened that the nation of the Picts, coming from Scythia, as it is reported, in a few ships, were driven by a storm entirely beyond all the coasts of Britain, and as far as the northern coasts of Ireland; where disembarking and finding the nation of the Scots, they requested to be allowed to settle amongst them, but could not obtain permission. (Ireland is the greatest island next to Britain, and situated to the westward of it.)

The Picts, arriving here, as I just now observed, petitioned the inhabitants to grant them permission to establish themselves as a colony amongst them. The Scots answered that the island was not large enough to contain them both; but we can give you good advice, added they; for we know there is another island, not far eastward from ours, which we can frequently see in clear weather. If you will go to it, you may easily establish yourselves there, or, if they should oppose you, employ us as auxiliaries. The Picts accordingly, sailing over to Britain, began to inhabit the northern parts of it; for the Britons were now possessed of the southern.

British Women c. 600 AD.

Now, these adventurers having brought no females with them, and applying to the Scots to allow them to marry with those of their nation, they would not consent to the proposal on any other terms than that, when any doubt should arise about the hereditary title to the crown, they should be bound to prefer the female line to the male, in the election of a king, which custom, it is well known, the Picts have always observed to this day.

In process of time, after the Britons and the Picts, Britain received a third nation, viz. the Scots, in that part which was possessed by the Picts. For these Scots coming out of Ireland, under the command of their leader Reuda, either by fair means, or by force of arms, entered and took possession of those places which they now inhabit. From which commander they are to this day called Dalreudins, Dal in their language signifying a part.

Ireland far surpasses Britain, both in breadth, and for its wholesome and serene air; so that snow scarcely ever lies on the ground more than three days together. No man makes hay in the summer for a winter's provision, or builds stables for his cattle. No noxious reptile is seen there, and no snake can live; for snakes have often been brought out of Britain for an experiment, and have been found dead as soon as the ships in which they were came near enough to the shore for them to be affected by the atmosphere. On the contrary, almost every thing which is brought from that island is an antidote against poison. In short, we have seen that when some persons have been stung by serpents, the scrapings of leaves of books that were brought out of Ireland, being put into water, and given them to drink, they immediately dispelled all the force of the spreading poison, and assuaged and took away all the tumours caused by the stings.

The island is well supplied with milk and honey, nor is there any want of fish or fowl, and it is remarkable for deer: there are also some vines. This is properly the country of the Scots. Coming out from thence as has been said, they added a third nation in Britain, to the Britons and Picts.

There is a large gulf, which formerly divided the nation of the Picts from the Britons; which gulf runs very far from the west into the land where, to this day, stands the very strong city of the Britons, called Alcuith. The Scots arriving on the north side of the bay, settled there.

Chapter Two

The first Invasion of Britain by the Romans, under Caius Julius Cæsar

Britain was neither resorted to nor known by the Romans till the time of Caius Julius Cæsar, who, in the year 593 [other MSS more accurately "693"; the accepted date is 699] from the building of Rome, the 60th before the birth of Christ, having been elected Consul with

Lucius Bibulus, whilst he conducted the war against the nations of the Germans and the Gauls, separated only by the river Rhine, came into the province of the Morini, from which, as we just now observed, is the shortest passage into this island. Here, having soon equipped a fleet of about 80 ships, large and small, he sailed over into Britain, where he at first met with a warm reception from the Britons, who made the most vigorous stand against him, and greatly harassed him. Afterwards being overtaken by a violent storm, he not only lost the greatest part of his fleet, but a great portion of his infantry, and almost all his cavalry.

Returning into France, he put his legions into winter quarters, and gave orders for building large and small ships of different descriptions, to the number of 600. Then, passing over again into Britain, he landed with an immense army, and attacked the Britons; but, whilst he was engaged in the battle, a sudden tempest arose, by which the ships, riding at anchor, were either dashed one against another, or driven on the sands; and 40 of them lost. The rest were with much difficulty repaired. Cæsar's cavalry was defeated by the enemy at the first charge, and here Labienus the tribune was killed: but Cæsar, renewing the attack after a great loss of his men, at length put the Britons to flight.

Thence he marched as far as the river Thames, which is said to be fordable only in one place. On the farther side of this river, an immense multitude of the enemy had assembled, under the command of Cassabelan their general; and fenced the bank, and almost all the ford under water, with very sharp stakes; the remains of which stakes are to be seen there to this day. They appear to be about the thickness of a man's leg, and being cased with lead, remain immovably fixed in the bottom of the river. The Romans having discovered this stratagem, avoided the danger by passing over the river at a little distance from them: which the Britons having perceived, and not daring to meet the shock of the Roman legions, fled into the neighbouring woods to conceal themselves; from which they afterwards frequently sallied out, and greatly harassed the Romans.

In the mean time, the strongest city of the Trinovantes (London), with Androgorius their general, surrendered to Cæsar, delivering forty hostages to him. This example was immediately followed by many other cities, which formed an alliance with the Romans. With their direction and assistance, Cæsar at length, with much difficulty, took Cassabelan's town, which was situated between two marshes, fortified by the surrounding woods, and furnished with all necessaries.

Roman Soldiers c. 150-200 A.D.

A Hymn of Glory Let Us Sing
by Bede (c. 731)

This hymn by Bede was translated by Benjamin Webb in 1854.

 hymn of glory let us sing
New songs throughout the world shall ring
Alleluia, Alleluia.
Christ, by a road before untrod
Ascendeth to the throne of God.
Alleluia, Alleluia, Alleluia, Alleluia, Alleluia.

The holy apostolic band
Upon the Mount of Olives stand
Alleluia, Alleluia.
And with His followers they see
Jesus' resplendent majesty
Alleluia, Alleluia, Alleluia, Alleluia, Alleluia.

To Whom the angels drawing nigh,
"Why stand and gaze upon the sky?"
Alleluia, Alleluia.
"This is the Savior," thus they say.
"This is His noble triumph day."
Alleluia, Alleluia, Alleluia, Alleluia, Alleluia.

"Again ye shall behold Him so,
As ye have today seen Him go."
Alleluia, Alleluia.
"In glorious pomp ascending high
Up to the portals of the sky."
Alleluia, Alleluia, Alleluia, Alleluia, Alleluia.

O God, Our Maker, Throned on High
attributed to King Alfred (c. 890)

This translation from Latin to English was made by Martin F. Tupper
and included in King Alfred's Poems, *published in 1850.*

King Alfred

O God, our Maker, throned on high,
The earth is Thine, and Thine the sky,
Th'adoring sun obeys Thy will,
And countless stars Thy laws fulfill.

The length'ning light of summer day,
The winter frost, Thy power display,
Nature proclaims Thy sovereign skill;
Man, and man only, spurns Thy will.

The wicked sit on earth's high seat,
And tread the holy 'neath their feet;
Good goes so crookedly astray,
Bright deeds lie hidden oft away.

Great God! Who seest from above,
Regard us with Thy pitying love,
Perplexed by doubts, with toil and strife,
We ask more light—we long for life.

O Sacred Head, Now Wounded
attributed to Bernard of Clairvaux (c. 1100s)

Clairvaux was born in his father's castle in 1109, the son of a knight.
He founded 163 monasteries. Martin Luther said he was
the best monk that ever lived.

O sacred Head, now wounded, with grief and shame weighed down,
Now scornfully surrounded with thorns, Thine only crown;
How pale Thou art with anguish, with sore abuse and scorn!
How does that visage languish, which once was bright as morn!

What Thou, my Lord, hast suffered, was all for sinners' gain;
Mine, mine was the transgression, but Thine the deadly pain.
Lo, here I fall, my Savior! 'Tis I deserve Thy place;
Look on me with Thy favor, vouchsafe to me Thy grace.

Men mock and taunt and jeer Thee, Thou noble countenance,
Though mighty worlds shall fear Thee and flee before Thy glance.
How art thou pale with anguish, with sore abuse and scorn!
How doth Thy visage languish that once was bright as morn!

Now from Thy cheeks has vanished their color once so fair;
From Thy red lips is banished the splendor that was there.
Grim death, with cruel rigor, hath robbed Thee of Thy life;
Thus Thou hast lost Thy vigor, Thy strength in this sad strife.

My burden in Thy Passion, Lord, Thou hast borne for me,
For it was my transgression which brought this woe on Thee.
I cast me down before Thee, wrath were my rightful lot;
Have mercy, I implore Thee; Redeemer, spurn me not!

What language shall I borrow to thank Thee, dearest friend,
For this Thy dying sorrow, Thy pity without end?
O make me Thine forever, and should I fainting be,
Lord, let me never, never outlive my love to Thee.

Bernard of Clairvaux

My Shepherd, now receive me; my Guardian, own me Thine.
Great blessings Thou didst give me, O source of gifts divine.
Thy lips have often fed me with words of truth and love;
Thy Spirit oft hath led me to heavenly joys above.

Here I will stand beside Thee, from Thee I will not part;
O Savior, do not chide me! When breaks Thy loving heart,
When soul and body languish in death's cold, cruel grasp,
Then, in Thy deepest anguish, Thee in mine arms I'll clasp.

The joy can never be spoken, above all joys beside,
When in Thy body broken I thus with safety hide.
O Lord of Life, desiring Thy glory now to see,
Beside Thy cross expiring, I'd breathe my soul to Thee.

My Savior, be Thou near me when death is at my door;
Then let Thy presence cheer me, forsake me nevermore!
When soul and body languish, oh, leave me not alone,
But take away mine anguish by virtue of Thine own!

Be Thou my consolation, my shield when I must die;
Remind me of Thy passion when my last hour draws nigh.
Mine eyes shall then behold Thee, upon Thy cross shall dwell,
My heart by faith enfolds Thee. Who dieth thus dies well.

Excerpts from The Magna Carta, Runnymeade, England (June 15, 1215)

An original copy of the Magna Carta is kept in the Chapter House of Salisbury Cathedral in Salisbury, England.

Preamble

John, by the grace of God, king of England, lord of Ireland, duke of Normandy and Aquitaine, and count of Anjou, to the archbishop, bishops, abbots, earls, barons, justiciaries, foresters, sheriffs, stewards, servants, and to all his bailiffs and liege subjects, greetings. Know that, having regard to God and for the salvation of our soul, and those of all our ancestors and heirs, and unto the honor of God and the advancement of his holy Church and for the rectifying of our realm, we have granted as underwritten by advice of our venerable fathers, Stephen, archbishop of Canterbury, primate of all England and cardinal of the holy Roman Church, Henry, archbishop of Dublin, William of London, Peter of Winchester, Jocelyn of Bath and Glastonbury, Hugh of Lincoln, Walter of Worcester, William of Coventry, Benedict of Rochester, bishops; of Master Pandulf, subdeacon and member of the household of our lord the Pope, of brother Aymeric (master of the Knights of the Temple in England), and of the illustrious men William Marshal, earl of Pembroke, William, earl of Salisbury, William, earl of Warenne, William, earl of Arundel, Alan of Galloway (constable of Scotland), Waren Fitz Gerold, Peter Fitz Herbert, Hubert De Burgh (seneschal of Poitou), Hugh de Neville, Matthew Fitz Herbert, Thomas Basset, Alan Basset, Philip d'Aubigny, Robert of Roppesley, John Marshal, John Fitz Hugh, and others, our liegemen.

1. In the first place we have granted to God, and by this our present charter confirmed for us and our heirs forever that the English Church shall be free, and shall have her rights entire, and her liberties inviolate; and we will that it be thus observed; which is apparent from this that the freedom of elections, which is reckoned most important and very essential to the English Church, we, of our pure and unconstrained will, did grant, and did by our charter confirm and did obtain the ratification of the same from our lord, Pope Innocent III, before the quarrel arose between us and our barons: and this we will observe, and our will is that it be observed in good faith by our heirs forever. We have also granted to all freemen of our

kingdom, for us and our heirs forever, all the underwritten liberties, to be had and held by them and their heirs, of us and our heirs forever.

6. Heirs shall be married without disparagement, yet so that before the marriage takes place the nearest in blood to that heir shall have notice.

7. A widow, after the death of her husband, shall forthwith and without difficulty have her marriage portion and inheritance; nor shall she give anything for her dower, or for her marriage portion, or for the inheritance which her husband and she held on the day of the death of that husband; and she may remain in the house of her husband for forty days after his death, within which time her dower shall be assigned to her.

8. No widow shall be compelled to marry, so long as she prefers to live without a husband; provided always that she gives security not to marry without our consent, if she holds of us, or without the consent of the lord of whom she holds, if she holds of another.

9. Neither we nor our bailiffs will seize any land or rent for any debt, as long as the chattels of the debtor are sufficient to repay the debt; nor shall the sureties of the debtor be distrained so long as the principal debtor is able to satisfy the debt; and if the principal debtor shall fail to pay the debt, having nothing wherewith to pay it, then the sureties shall answer for the debt; and let them have the lands and rents of the debtor, if they desire them, until they are indemnified for the debt which they have paid for him, unless the principal debtor can show proof that he is discharged thereof as against the said sureties.

10. If one who has borrowed from the Jews any sum, great or small, die before that loan be repaid, the debt shall not bear interest while the heir is under age, of whomsoever he may hold; and if the debt fall into our hands, we will not take anything except the principal sum contained in the bond.

11. And if anyone die indebted to the Jews, his wife shall have her dower and pay nothing of that debt; and if any children of the deceased are left under age, necessaries shall be provided for them in keeping with the holding of the deceased; and out of the residue the debt shall be paid, reserving, however, service due to feudal lords; in like manner let it be done touching debts due to others than Jews.

12. No scutage [monetary payments to replace military service] nor aid [tax] shall be imposed on our kingdom, unless by common counsel of our kingdom, except for ransoming our person, for making our eldest son a knight, and for once marrying our eldest daughter; and for these there shall not be levied more than a reasonable aid. In like manner it shall be done concerning aids from the city of London.

13. And the city of London shall have all its ancient liberties and free customs, as well by land as by water; furthermore, we decree and grant that all other cities, boroughs, towns, and ports shall have all their liberties and free customs.

14. And for obtaining the common counsel of the kingdom anent the assessing of an aid (except in the three cases aforesaid) or of a scutage, we will cause to be summoned the archbishops, bishops, abbots, earls, and greater barons, severally by our letters; and we will moreover cause to be summoned generally, through our sheriffs and bailiffs, and others who hold of us in chief, for a fixed date, namely, after the expiry of at least forty days, and at a fixed place; and in all letters of such summons we will specify the reason of the summons. And when the summons has thus been made, the business shall proceed on the day appointed, according to the counsel of such as are present, although not all who were summoned have come.

15. We will not for the future grant to anyone license to take an aid from his own free tenants, except to ransom his person, to make his eldest son a knight, and once to marry his eldest daughter; and on each of these occasions there shall be levied only a reasonable aid.

16. No one shall be distrained for performance of greater service for a knight's fee, or for any other free tenement, than is due therefrom.

17. Common pleas shall not follow our court, but shall be held in some fixed place.

18. Inquests of novel disseisin, of mort d'ancestor, and of darrein presentment shall not be held elsewhere than in their own county courts, and that in manner following; We, or, if we should be out of the realm, our chief justiciar, will send two justiciaries through every county four times a year, who shall alone with four knights of the county chosen by the county, hold the said assizes in the county court, on the day and in the place of meeting of that court.

Interior of Salisbury Cathedral

20. A freeman shall not be amerced [fined or punished] for a slight offense, except in accordance with the degree of the offense; and for a grave offense he shall be amerced in accordance with the gravity of the offense, yet saving always his "contentment"; and a merchant in the same way, saving his "merchandise"; and a villein shall be amerced in the same way, saving his "wainage" if they have fallen into our mercy: and none of the aforesaid amercements shall be imposed except by the oath of honest men of the neighborhood.

21. Earls and barons shall not be amerced except through their peers, and only in accordance with the degree of the offense.

23. No village or individual shall be compelled to make bridges at river banks, except those who from of old were legally bound to do so.

28. No constable or other bailiff of ours shall take corn or other provisions from anyone without immediately tendering money therefor, unless he can have postponement thereof by permission of the seller.

29. No constable shall compel any knight to give money in lieu of castle-guard, when he is willing to perform it in his own person, or (if he himself cannot do it from any reasonable cause) then by another responsible man. Further, if we have led or sent him upon military service, he shall be relieved from guard in proportion to the time during which he has been on service because of us.

30. No sheriff or bailiff of ours, or other person, shall take the horses or carts of any freeman for transport duty, against the will of the said freeman.

31. Neither we nor our bailiffs shall take, for our castles or for any other work of ours, wood which is not ours, against the will of the owner of that wood.

32. We will not retain beyond one year and one day, the lands of those who have been convicted of felony, and the lands shall thereafter be handed over to the lords of the fiefs.

35. Let there be one measure of wine throughout our whole realm; and one measure of ale; and one measure of corn, to wit, "the London quarter"; and one width of cloth (whether dyed, or russet, or "halberget"), to wit, two ells within the selvedges; of weights also let it be as of measures.

38. No bailiff for the future shall, upon his own unsupported complaint, put anyone to his "law", without credible witnesses brought for this purpose.

40. To no one will we sell, to no one will we refuse or delay, right or justice.

41. All merchants shall have safe and secure exit from England, and entry to England, with the right to tarry there and to move about as well by land as by water, for buying and selling by the ancient and right customs, quit from all evil tolls, except (in time of war) such merchants as are of the land at war with us. And if such are found in our land at the beginning of the war, they shall be detained, without injury to their bodies or goods, until information be received by us, or by our chief justiciar, how the merchants of our land found in the land at war with us are treated; and if our men are safe there, the others shall be safe in our land.

42. It shall be lawful in future for anyone (excepting always those imprisoned or outlawed in accordance with the law of the kingdom, and natives of any country at war with us, and merchants, who shall be treated as if above provided) to leave our kingdom and to return, safe and secure by land and water, except for a short period in time of war, on grounds of public policy, reserving always the allegiance due to us.

45. We will appoint as justices, constables, sheriffs, or bailiffs only such as know the law of the realm and mean to observe it well.

46. All barons who have founded abbeys, concerning which they hold charters from the kings of England, or of which they have long continued possession, shall have the wardship of them, when vacant, as they ought to have.

54. No one shall be arrested or imprisoned upon the appeal of a woman, for the death of any other than her husband.

55. All fines made with us unjustly and against the law of the land, and all amercements, imposed unjustly and against the law of the land, shall be entirely remitted, or else it shall be done concerning them according to the decision of the five and twenty barons whom mention is made below in the clause for securing the peace, or according to the judgment of the majority of the same, along with the aforesaid Stephen, archbishop of Canterbury, if he can be present, and such others as he may wish to bring with him for this purpose, and if he cannot be present the business shall nevertheless proceed without him, provided always that if any one or more of the aforesaid five and twenty barons are in a similar suit, they shall be removed as far as concerns this particular judgment, others being substituted in their places after having been selected by the rest of the same five and twenty for this purpose only, and after having been sworn.

56. If we have disseised or removed Welshmen from lands or liberties, or other things, without the legal judgment of their peers in England or in Wales, they shall be immediately restored to them; and if a dispute arise over this, then let it be decided in the marches by the judgment of their peers; for the tenements in England according to the law of England, for tenements in Wales according to the law of Wales, and for tenements in the marches according to the law of the marches. Welshmen shall do the same to us and ours.

61. Since, moreover, for God and the amendment of our kingdom and for the better allaying of the quarrel that has arisen between us and our barons, we have granted all these concessions, desirous that they should enjoy them in complete and firm endurance forever, we give and grant to them the underwritten security, namely, that the barons choose five and twenty barons of the kingdom, whomsoever they will, who shall be bound with all their might, to observe and hold, and cause to be observed, the peace and liberties we have granted and confirmed to them by this our present Charter, so that if we, or our justiciar, or our bailiffs or any one of our officers, shall in anything be at fault towards anyone, or shall have broken any one of the articles of this peace or of this security, and the offense be notified to four barons of the foresaid five and twenty, the said four barons shall repair to us (or our justiciar, if we are out of the realm) and, laying the transgression before us, petition to have that transgression redressed without delay. And if we shall not have corrected the transgression

(or, in the event of our being out of the realm, if our justiciar shall not have corrected it) within forty days, reckoning from the time it has been intimated to us (or to our justiciar, if we should be out of the realm), the four barons aforesaid shall refer that matter to the rest of the five and twenty barons, and those five and twenty barons shall, together with the community of the whole realm, distrain and distress us in all possible ways, namely, by seizing our castles, lands, possessions, and in any other way they can, until redress has been obtained as they deem fit, saving harmless our own person, and the persons of our queen and children; and when redress has been obtained, they shall resume their old relations towards us.

62. And all the will, hatreds, and bitterness that have arisen between us and our men, clergy and lay, from the date of the quarrel, we have completely remitted and pardoned to everyone. Moreover, all trespasses occasioned by the said quarrel, from Easter in the sixteenth year of our reign till the restoration of peace, we have fully remitted to all, both clergy and laymen, and completely forgiven, as far as pertains to us. And on this head, we have caused to be made for them letters testimonial patent of the lord Stephen, archbishop of Canterbury, of the lord Henry, archbishop of Dublin, of the bishops aforesaid, and of Master Pandulf as touching this security and the concessions aforesaid.

63. Wherefore we will and firmly order that the English Church be free, and that the men in our kingdom have and hold all the aforesaid liberties, rights, and concessions, well and peaceably, freely and quietly, fully and wholly, for themselves and their heirs, of us and our heirs, in all respects and in all places forever, as is aforesaid. An oath, moreover, has been taken, as well on our part as on the part of the barons, that all these conditions aforesaid shall be kept in good faith and without evil intent.

Given under our hand—the above named and many others being witnesses—in the meadow which is called Runnymede, between Windsor and Staines, on the fifteenth day of June, in the seventeenth year of our reign.

Canterbury

All Creatures of Our God and King
by Francis of Assisi (c. 1225)

Francis of Assisi wrote this hymn shortly before his death in 1226. It was not published until the 1600s. This English translation was completed by English minister and hymn writer William H. Draper for a children's festival in Leeds, England. His translation was included in the Public School Hymn Book, published in 1919.

All creatures of our God and King
Lift up your voice and with us sing,
Alleluia! Alleluia!
Thou burning sun with golden beam,
Thou silver moon with softer gleam!

Refrain (sung after each verse)
O praise Him! O praise Him!
Alleluia! Alleluia! Alleluia!

Thou rushing wind that art so strong
Ye clouds that sail in Heaven along,
O praise Him! Alleluia!
Thou rising moon, in praise rejoice,
Ye lights of evening, find a voice!

Thou flowing water, pure and clear,
Make music for thy Lord to hear,
O praise Him! Alleluia!
Thou fire so masterful and bright,
That givest man both warmth and light.

And all ye men of tender heart,
Forgiving others, take your part,
O sing ye! Alleluia!
Ye who long pain and sorrow bear,
Praise God and on Him cast your care!

And thou most kind and gentle Death,
Waiting to hush our latest breath,
O praise Him! Alleluia!
Thou leadest home the child of God,
And Christ our Lord the way hath trod.

Let all things their Creator bless,
And worship Him in humbleness,
O praise Him! Alleluia!
Praise, praise the Father, praise the Son,
And praise the Spirit, Three in One!

Francis of Assisi

Dost Thou Truly Seek Renown?
by Louis IX (c. 1239)

King Louis IX of France evidently wrote this hymn for the Office of the Reception of the Holy Crown festival, which was first celebrated in Paris in 1239. It was translated into English by J. Athelstan Riley and published in Songs of Syon *in 1904.*

Dost thou truly seek renown
Christ His glory sharing?
Wouldst thou win the heavenly crown
Victor's meed declaring?
Tread the path the Savior trod,
Look upon the crown of God,
See what He is wearing.

This the King of Heaven bore
In that sore contending;
This His sacred temples wore,
Honor to it lending;
In this helm He faced the foe,
On the rood He laid him low,
Satan's kingdom ending.

Christ upon the tree of scorn,
In salvation's hour,
Turned to gold those pricks of thorn
By His Passion's power;
So on sinners, who had earned
Endless death, from sin returned,
Endless blessings shower.

When in death's embrace we lie,
Then, good Lord, be near us;
With Thy presence fortify,
And with victory cheer us;
Turn our erring hearts to Thee,
That we crowned for ay may be:
O good Jesu, hear us!

Louis IX

Everyman

Anonymous (late 1400s)

*This edition of this morality play is based on the edition in
"A Select Collection of Old English Plays, Volume I," published by W. Carew Hazlitt in 1873.*

DRAMATIS PERSONAE

MESSENGER	KNOWLEDGE
GOD	CONFESSION
DEATH	BEAUTY
EVERYMAN	STRENGTH
FELLOWSHIP	DISCRETION
KINDRED	FIVE WITS
COUSIN	ANGEL
GOODS	DOCTOR
GOOD DEEDS	

HERE BEGINNETH A TREATISE HOW THE HIGH FATHER OF HEAVEN SENDETH DEATH TO SUMMON EVERY CREATURE TO COME AND GIVE ACCOUNT OF THEIR LIVES IN THIS WORLD, AND IS IN MANNER OF A MORAL PLAY.

MESSENGER.
I Pray you all give your audience,
And hear this matter with reverence,
By figure a moral play;
The Summoning of Everyman called it is,
That of our lives and ending shows,
How transitory we be all day:
This matter is wondrous precious,
But the intent of it is more gracious,
And sweet to bear away.
The story saith: man, in the beginning
Look well, and take good heed to the ending,
Be you never so gay:
Ye think sin in the beginning full sweet,
Which in the end causeth thy soul to weep,
When the body lieth in clay.
Here shall you see how Fellowship and Jollity,
Both Strength, Pleasure, and Beauty,
Will fade from thee as flower in May;
For ye shall hear, how our Heaven King
Calleth Everyman to a general reckoning:
Give audience, and hear what he doth say.

GOD *speaketh*.
I perceive here in my Majesty,
How that all creatures be to me unkind,
Living without dread in worldly prosperity:
Of ghostly sight the people be so blind,
Drowned in sin, they knew me not for their God;
In worldly riches is all their mind,
They fear not my rightwiseness, the sharp rod;
My law that I showed, when I for them died,
They forget clean, and shedding of my blood red;
I hanged between two, it cannot be denied;
To get them life I suffered to be dead;
I healed their feet, with thorns hurt was my head:
I could do no more than I did truly,
And now I see the people do clean forsake me:
They use the seven deadly sins damnable,
As pride, covetise, wrath, and lechery,
Now in the world be made commendable:
And thus they leave, of angels the
   heavenly company,
Every man liveth so after his own pleasure,
And yet of their life they be nothing sure:
I see the more that I them forbear
The worse they be from year to year;

Woodcut illustration of Everyman

All that liveth appaireth[1] fast,
Therefore I will in all the haste
Have a reckoning of every man's person;
For, and I leave the people thus alone
In their life and wicked tempests,
Verily they will become much worse than beasts;
For now one would by envy another up eat;
Charity they do all clean forget.
I hoped well that every man
In my glory should make his mansion,
And thereto I had them all elect;
But now I see, like traitors deject,
They thank me not for the pleasure that I to
    them meant,
Nor yet for their being that I them have lent;
I proffered the people great multitude of mercy,
And few there be that asketh it heartly;
They be so cumbered with worldly riches,
That needs on them I must do justice,
On every man living without fear.
Where art thou, Death, thou mighty messenger?

DEATH.
Almighty God, I am here at your will,
Your commandment to fulfil.

GOD.
Go thou to Everyman,
And show him in my name
A pilgrimage he must on him take,
Which he in no wise may escape;
And that he bring with him a sure reckoning
Without delay or any tarrying.

DEATH.
Lord, I will in the world go run over all,
And cruelly out-search both great and small;
Every man will I beset that liveth beastly,
Out of God's laws, and dreadeth not folly:
He that loveth riches I will strike with my dart,
His sight to blind, and from heaven to depart,

Except that alms be his good friend,
In hell for to dwell, world without end.
Lo, yonder I see Everyman walking:
Full little he thinketh on my coming:
His mind is on fleshly lusts and his treasure;
And great pain it shall cause him to endure
Before the Lord, heaven's King.
Everyman, stand still; whither art thou going
Thus gaily? hast thou thy Maker forgot?

EVERYMAN.
Why askest thou? Wouldest thou wit?

DEATH.
Yea, sir, I will show you; in great haste
    I am sent to thee
From God out of his Majesty.

EVERYMAN.
What! sent to me?

DEATH.
Yea, certainly:
Though thou have forget him here,
He thinketh on thee in the heavenly sphere;
As, ere we depart, thou shalt know.

EVERYMAN.
What desireth God of me?

DEATH.
That shall I show thee;
A reckoning he will needs have
Without any longer respite.

EVERYMAN.
To give a reckoning longer leisure I crave;
This blind matter troubleth my wit.

DEATH.
On thee thou must take a long journey,
Therefore thy book of count with thee thou bring,

---

[1] grows worse, degenerates

For turn again thou cannot by no way:
And look thou be sure of thy reckoning;
For before God thou shalt answer and show
Thy many bad deeds, and good but a few,
How thou hast spent thy life, and in what wise,
Before the chief lord of paradise.
Have ado that we were in that way,
For, wit thou well, thou shalt make none attorney.[2]

EVERYMAN.
Full unready I am such reckoning to give:
I know thee not; what messenger art thou?

DEATH.
I am Death, that no man dreadeth;
For every man I 'rrest, and no man spareth,
For it is God's commandment
That all to me should be obedient.

EVERYMAN.
O Death, thou comest, when I had thee
   least in mind;
In thy power it lieth me to save;
Yet of my good will I give thee, if thou
    will be kind,
Yea, a thousand pounds shalt thou have,
And defer this matter till another day.

DEATH.
Everyman, it may not be by no way;
I set not by gold, silver, nor riches,
Ne[3] by pope, emperor, king, duke, ne princes;
For, and I would receive gifts great,
All the world I might get;
But my custom is clean contrary;
I give thee no respite, come hence, and not tarry.

EVERYMAN.
Alas! shall I have no lenger respite?
I may say Death giveth no warning:

To think on thee it maketh my heart sick;
For all unready is my book of reckoning:
But, twelve year and I might have abiding,
My counting-book I would make so clear,
That my reckoning I should not need to fear.
Wherefore, Death, I pray thee for God's mercy,
Spare me, till I be provided of remedy.

DEATH.
Thee availeth not to cry, weep, and pray:
But haste thee lightly, that thou wert gone
   this journey;
And prove thy friends, if thou can;
For, wit thou well, the tide abideth no man,
And in the world each living creature
For Adam's sin must die of nature.

EVERYMAN.
Death, if I should this pilgrimage take,
And my reckoning surely make,
Show me, for Saint Charity,[4]
Should I not come again shortly?

DEATH.
No, Everyman, and thou be once there,
Thou mayest never more come here,
Trust me verily.

EVERYMAN.
O gracious God, in the high seat celestial,
Have mercy on me in this most need.
Shall I have no company from this vale terrestrial
Of mine acquaintance, that way me to lead?

---

[2] You cannot get a mediator.
[3] nor

[4] In Catholic tradition, Charity was persecuted with her sisters and mother during the reign of Hadrian.

DEATH.
Yea, if any be so hardy,
That would go with thee, and bear thee company:
Hie[5] thee that thou were gone to
    God's magnificence,
Thy reckoning to give before his presence.
What, weenest[6] thou thy life is given thee,
And thy worldly goods also?

EVERYMAN.
I had ween'd so verily.

DEATH.
Nay, nay; it was but lent thee;
For, as soon as thou art gone,
Another awhile shall have it, and then go therefro,
Even as thou hast done.
Everyman, thou art mad, thou hast thy wits five,[7]
And here on earth will not amend thy life;
For suddenly I do come.

EVERYMAN.
O wretched caitiff,[8] whither shall I flee,
That I might escape this endless sorrow!
Now, gentle Death, spare me till to-morrow,
That I may amend me
With good advisement.

DEATH.
Nay, thereto I will not consent,
Nor no man will I respite;
But to the heart suddenly I shall smite
Without any advisement.
And now out of thy sight I will me hie;
See thou make thee ready shortly,
For thou mayest say, this is the day
That no man living may 'scape away.

---

[5] hurry, make haste

[6] think, suppose

[7] In medieval thought, the five wits included common sense, imagination, fantasy, estimation, and memory.

[8] despicable person

EVERYMAN.
Alas! I may well weep with sighs deep:
Now have I no manner of company
To help me in my journey, and me to keep;
And also my writing is full unready.
How shall I do now for to excuse me!
I would to God I had never be gete;[9]
To my soul a full great profit it had be;
For now I fear pains huge and great.
The time passeth: Lord, help, that all wrought!
For though I mourn, it availeth nought:
The day passeth, and is almost ago;
I wot not well what for to do.
To whom were I best my complaint to make?
What, and I to Fellowship thereof spake,
And showed him of this sudden chance!
For in him is all mine affiance;
We have in the world so many a day
Be good friends in sport and play,
I see him yonder certainly;
I trust that he will bear me company,
Therefore to him will I speak to ease my sorrow,
Well met, good Fellowship, and good morrow.

FELLOWSHIP *speaketh*.
Everyman, good morrow, by this day:
Sir, why lookest thou so piteously?
If anything be amiss, I pray thee, me say,
That I may help to remedy.

EVERYMAN.
Yea, good Fellowship, yea;
I am in great jeopardy.

FELLOWSHIP.
My true friend, show to me your mind;
I will not forsake thee, to my life's end,
In the way of good company.

EVERYMAN.
That was well spoken and lovingly.

---

[9] been begotten, been born

56

FELLOWSHIP.
Sir, I must needs know your heaviness;
I have pity to see you in any distress:
If any have you wronged, ye shall revenged be,
Though I on the ground be slain for thee;
Though that I know before that I should die.

EVERYMAN.
Verily, Fellowship, gramercy.[10]

FELLOWSHIP.
Tush! by thy thanks I set not a straw;
Show me your grief, and say no more.

EVERYMAN.
If I my heart should to you break,
And then you to turn your mind from me,
And would not me comfort, when ye
   hear me speak,
Then should I ten times sorrier be.

FELLOWSHIP.
Sir, I say as I will do in deed.

EVERYMAN.
Then be you a good friend at need;
I have found you true here-before.

FELLOWSHIP.
And so ye shall evermore;
For in faith, and thou go to hell,
I will not forsake thee by the way.

EVERYMAN.
Ye speak like a good friend, I believe you well;
I shall deserve it, and I may.

FELLOWSHIP.
I speak of no deserving, by this day;
For he that will say and nothing do,
Is not worthy with good company to go:
Therefore show me the grief of your mind,
As to your friend most loving and kind.

EVERYMAN.
I shall show you how it is:
Commanded I am to go a journey,
A long way, hard and dangerous;
And give a strait account without delay
Before the High Judge Adonai;
Wherefore, I pray you, bear me company,
As ye have promised in this journey.

FELLOWSHIP.
That is matter indeed; promise is duty;
But, and I should take such a voyage on me,
I know it well, it should be to my pain:
Also it make me afeard certain.
But let us take counsel here as well as we can,
For your words would fear a strong man.

EVERYMAN.
Why, ye said, if I had need,
Ye would me never forsake, quick ne dead,
Though it were to hell truly.

FELLOWSHIP.
So I said certainly;
But such pleasures be set aside, the sooth to say,
And also if we took such a journey,
When should we come again?

EVERYMAN.
Nay, never again till the day of doom.

FELLOWSHIP.
In faith, then will not I come there:
Who hath you these tidings brought?

---

[10] grand mercy (great thanks)

EVERYMAN.
Indeed, Death was with me here.

FELLOWSHIP.
Now, by God that all hath bought,
If Death were the messenger,
For no man that is living to-day
I will not go that loath journey,
Not for the father that begat me.

EVERYMAN.
Ye promised otherwise, pardy.[11]

FELLOWSHIP.
I wot well I said so truly,
And yet if thou wilt eat and drink,
    and make good cheer,
Or haunt to women the lusty company,
I would not forsake you, while the day is clear,
Trust me verily.

EVERYMAN.
Yea, thereto ye would be ready;
To go to mirth, solace and play,
Your mind will sooner apply
Than to bear me company in my long journey.

FELLOWSHIP.
Now, in good faith, I will not that way;
But, and thou will murder, or any man kill,
In that I will help thee with a good will.

EVERYMAN.
Oh, that is a simple advice indeed:
Gentle fellow, help me in my necessity;
We have loved long, and now I need,
And now, gentle Fellowship, remember me.

FELLOWSHIP.
Whether ye have loved me or no,
By Saint John, I will not with thee go.

EVERYMAN.
Yet, I pray thee, take the labour,
    and do so much for me,
To bring me forward, for Saint Charity,
And comfort me, till I come without the town.

FELLOWSHIP.
Nay, and thou would give me a new gown,
I will not a foot with thee go;
But, and thou had tarried, I would not have
    left thee so:
And as now God speed thee in thy journey!
For from thee I will depart, as fast as I may.

EVERYMAN.
Whither away, Fellowship? will you forsake me?

FELLOWSHIP.
Yea, by my fay;[12] to God I betake thee.

EVERYMAN.
Farewell, good Fellowship; for this
    my heart is sore:
Adieu for ever, I shall see thee no more.

FELLOWSHIP.
In faith, Everyman, farewell now at the end;
For you I will remember that
    parting is mourning.

EVERYMAN.
Alack! shall we thus depart in deed,
Our Lady, help, without any more comfort,
Lo, Fellowship forsaketh me in my most need:
For help in this world whither shall I resort?
Fellowship here before with me
    would merry make;
And now little sorrow for me doth he take.
It is said, in prosperity men friends may find,
Which in adversity be full unkind.
Now whither for succour shall I flee,

---

[11] exclamation meaning "by God"

[12] faith

Sith[13] that Fellowship hath forsaken me?
To my kinsmen I will truly,
Praying them to help me in my necessity;
I believe that they will do so;
For kind will creep, where it may not go.
I will go say; for yonder I see them go:
Where be ye now, my friends and kinsmen?

KINDRED.
Here be we now at your commandment:
Cousin, I pray thee, show us your intent
In any wise, and do not spare.

COUSIN.
Yea, Everyman, and to us declare
If ye be disposed to go any whither;
For, wot ye well, we will live and die together.

KINDRED.
In wealth and woe we will with you hold;
For over his kin a man may be bold.

EVERYMAN.
Gramercy, my friends and kinsmen kind,
Now shall I show you the grief of my mind.
I was commanded by a messenger,
That is an high king's chief officer;
He bad me go on pilgrimage to my pain,
But I know well I shall never come again:
Also I must give a reckoning strait;
For I have a great enemy that hath me in wait,
Which intendeth me for to hinder.

KINDRED.
What account is that which ye must render?
That would I know.

EVERYMAN.
Of all my works I must show,
How I have lived, and my days spent;

Also of ill deeds that I have used
In my time, sith life was me lent,
And of all virtues that I have refused:
Therefore, I pray you, go thither with me
To help to make mine account, for Saint Charity.

COUSIN.
What, to go thither? Is that the matter?
Nay, Everyman, I had liever[14] fast bread
        and water,
All this five year and more.

EVERYMAN.
Alas, that ever I was bore![15]
For now shall I never be merry,
If that you forsake me.

KINDRED.
Ah, sir! what, ye be a merry man!
Take good heart to you, and make no moan.
But one thing I warn you, by Saint Anne,
As for me ye shall go alone.

EVERYMAN.
My cousin, will you not with me go?

COUSIN.
No, by our lady, I have the cramp in my toe:
Trust not to me; for, so God me speed,
I will deceive you in your most need.

KINDRED.
It availeth not us to tice:[16]
Ye shall have my maid with all my heart;
She loveth to go to feasts, there to be nice,
And to dance, and abroad to start:
I will give her leave to help you in that journey,
If that you and she may agree.

---

13 since, now that

14 rather
15 born
16 entice

EVERYMAN.

No, show me the very effect of your mind;

Will you go with me, or abide behind?

KINDRED.

Abide behind! yea, that will I, and I may;

Therefore farewell till another day.

EVERYMAN.

How should I be merry or glad?

For fair promises men to me make;

But, when I have most need, they me forsake;

I am deceived, that maketh me sad.

COUSIN.

Cousin Everyman, farewell now;

For verily I will not go with you:

Also of mine own life an unready reckoning

I have to account, therefore I make tarrying;

Now God keep thee, for now I go.

EVERYMAN.

Ah, Jesu,[17] is all come hereto?

Lo, fair words maketh fools fain;

They promise, and nothing will do certain.

My kinsmen promised me faithfully,

For to abide with me steadfastly;

And now fast away do they flee:

Even so Fellowship promised me.

What friend were best me of to provide?

I lose my time here longer to abide;

Yet in my mind a thing there is:

All my life I have loved riches;

If that my Good now help me might,

It would make my heart full light:

I will speak to him in this distress:

Where art thou, my Goods and Riches?

GOODS.

Who calleth me? Everyman?

    what, hast thou haste?

I lie here in corners trussed and piled so high,

And in chests I am locked so fast,

Also sacked in bags, thou mayest

    see with thine eye,

I cannot stir; in packs, lo, where I lie!

What would ye have, lightly me say.

EVERYMAN.

Come hither, Good, in all the haste thou may;

For of counsel I must desire thee.

GOODS.

Sir, and ye in the world have sorrow or adversity,

That can I help you to remedy shortly.

EVERYMAN.

It is another disease that grieveth me;

In this world it is not, I tell thee so,

I am sent for another way to go,

To give a strait account general

Before the highest Jupiter of all:

And all my life I have had my pleasure in thee,

Therefore I pray thee now go with me;

For, peraventure, thou mayest before

    God Almighty

My reckoning help to clean and purify,

For it is said ever among,

That money maketh all right that is wrong.

---

[17] Jesus

GOODS.

Nay, nay, Everyman, I sing another song;
I follow no man in such voyages,
For, and I went with thee,
Thou shouldest fare much the worse for me:
For because on me thou diddest set thy mind,
Thy reckoning I have made blotted and blind,
That thine account thou cannot make truly;
And that hast thou for the love of me.

EVERYMAN.

That would grieve me full sore,
When I should come to that fearful answer:
Up, and let us go thither together.

GOODS.

Nay, not so; I am too brittle, I may not endure:
I will follow no man one foot, be ye sure.

EVERYMAN.

Alas! I have thee loved, and had great pleasure
All my life-days on my good and treasure.

GOODS.

That is to thy damnation without lesing,[18]
For my love is contrary to the love everlasting;
But if thou had me loved moderately during,
As to the poor give part for the love of me,
Then shouldest thou not in this dolour have be,
Nor in this great sorrow and care.

EVERYMAN.

Lo, now was I deceived, ere I was ware,
And all, I may wete, mis-spending of time.

GOODS.

What, wenest thou that I am thine?

EVERYMAN.

I had wend so.

GOODS.

Nay, Everyman, I say no:
As for a while I was lent thee;
A season thou hast had me in prosperity;
My condition is man's soul to kill,
If I save one, a thousand I do spill:
Weenest thou that I will follow thee?
Nay, not from this world, verily.

EVERYMAN.

I had wend otherwise.

GOODS.

Therefore to thy soul Good is a thief,
For when thou art dead, this is my guise,
Another to deceive in the same wise,
As I have do thee, and all to his soul's reprefe.[19]

EVERYMAN.

O false Good, cursed may thou be,
Thou traitor to God, thou hast deceived me,
And caught me in thy snare.

GOODS.

Marry, thou brought thyself in care,
Whereof I am right glad:
I must needs laugh, I cannot be sad.

EVERYMAN.

Ah, Good, thou hast had long my hearty love;
I gave thee that which should be the Lord's above:
But wilt thou not go with me indeed?
I pray thee truth to say.

GOODS.

No, so God me speed;
Therefore farewell, and have good day.

---

[18] lying

[19] reproach, blame

EVERYMAN.
Oh, to whom shall I make my moan,
For to go with me in that heavy journey?
First Fellowship he said he would with me gone;
His words were very pleasant and gay,
But afterward he left me alone.
Then spake I to my kinsmen all in despair,
And also they gave me words fair,
They lacked no fair speaking;
But all forsake me in the ending.
Then went I to my Goods that I loved best,
In hope to have found comfort;
   but there had I least:
For my Goods sharply did me tell,
That he bringeth many in hell.
Then of myself I was ashamed,
And so I am worthy to be blamed:
Thus may I well myself hate.
Of whom shall I now counsel take?
I think that I shall never speed,
Till that I go to my Good Deed;
But, alas! she is so weak,
That she can neither go nor speak:
Yet will I venture on her now.
My Good Deeds, where be you?

GOOD DEEDS.
Here I lie cold in the ground;
Thy sins have me so sore bound,
That I cannot stir.

EVERYMAN.
O Good Deeds, I stand in great fear;
I must you pray of counsel,
For help now should come right well.

GOOD DEEDS.
Everyman, I have understanding,
That thou art summoned account to make
Before Messias of Jerusalem King;
And you do by me, that journey with you
   will I take.

EVERYMAN.
Therefore I come to you my moan to make:
I pray you, that ye will go with me.

GOOD DEEDS.
I would full fain, but I cannot stand verily.

EVERYMAN.
Why, is there anything on you fall?

GOOD DEEDS.
Yea, sir, I may thank you of all;
If ye had perfectly cheered me,
Your book of account full ready now had be.
Look, the books of your works and deeds eke![20]
Behold how they lie under the feet,
To your soul's heaviness.

EVERYMAN.
Our Lord Jesus help me,
For one letter herein can I not see.

GOOD DEEDS.
Here is a blind reckoning in time of distress!

EVERYMAN.
Good Deeds, I pray you, help me in this need,
Or else I am for ever damned indeed;
Therefore help me to make my reckoning
Before the Redeemer of all thing,
That king is, and was, and ever shall.

GOOD DEEDS.
Everyman, I am sorry of your fall,
And fain would I help you, and I were able.

EVERYMAN.
Good Deeds, your counsel, I pray you, give me.

------

[20] also

62

GOOD DEEDS.
That shall I do verily:
Though that on my feet I may not go,
I have a sister that shall with you also,
Called Knowledge, which shall with you abide,
To help you to make that dreadful reckoning.
              [*Enter Knowledge.*

KNOWLEDGE.
Everyman, I will go with thee, and be thy guide,
In thy most need to go by thy side.

EVERYMAN.
In good condition I am now in every thing,
And am wholly content with this good thing,
Thanked be God my Creator.

GOOD DEEDS.
And when he hath brought thee there,
Where thou shalt heal thee of thy smart,
Then go thou with thy reckoning and
      thy good deeds together.
For to make thee joyful at the heart
Before the blessed Trinity.

EVERYMAN.
My Good Deeds, I thank thee heartfully:
I am well content certainly
With your words sweet.

KNOWLEDGE.
Now go we together lovingly
To Confession, that cleansing river.

EVERYMAN.
For joy I weep: I would we there were;
But I pray you to instruct me by intellection,[21]
Where dwelleth that holy virtue Confession?

KNOWLEDGE.
In the house of salvation;
We shall find him in that place,
That shall us comfort by God's grace.
Lo, this is Confession: kneel down, and ask mercy;
For he is in good conceit[22] with God Almighty.

EVERYMAN.
O glorious fountain that all uncleanness
      doth clarify,
Wash from me the spots of vices unclean,
That on me no sin may be seen;
I come with Knowledge for my redemption,
Redempt with heart and full contrition,
For I am commanded a pilgrimage to take,
And great accounts before God to make.
Now I pray you, Shrift,[23] mother of salvation,
Help hither my good deeds for my piteous
      exclamation.

_____
[21] knowledge

_____
[22] opinion, estimation
[23] confession

CONFESSION.
I know your sorrow well, Everyman:
Because with Knowledge ye come to me,
I will you comfort as well as I can;
And a precious jewel I will give thee,
Called penance, voider of adversity:
Therewith shall your body chastised be
With abstinence and perseverance in God's service;
Here shall you receive that scourge of me,
Which is penance strong that ye must endure,
Remember thy Saviour was scourged for thee
With sharp scourges, and suffered it patiently:
So must thou, ere thou pass thy pilgrimage.
Knowledge, keep him in this voyage,
And by that time Good Deeds will be with thee;
But in anywise be sure of mercy,
For your time draweth fast; and ye will saved be,
Ask God mercy, and he will grant truly:
When with the scourge of penance
    man doth him bind,
The oil of forgiveness then shall he find.

EVERYMAN.
Thanked be God for his gracious work;
For now I will my penance begin:
This hath rejoiced and lighted my heart,
Though the knots be painful and hard within.

KNOWLEDGE.
Everyman, look your penance that ye fulfil,
What pain that ever it to you be;
And I shall give you counsel at will,
How your account ye shall make clearly.

EVERYMAN.
O eternal God, O heavenly figure,
O way of rightwiseness, O goodly vision,
Which descended down in a virgin pure,
Because he would Everyman redeem,
Which Adam forfeited by his disobedience,
O blessed Godhead, elect and high Divine,
Forgive me my grievous offence;

Here I cry thee mercy in this presence:
O ghostly treasure, O ransomer and redeemer!
Of all the world hope and conductor,
Mirror of joy, foundation of mercy,
Which enlumineth heaven and earth thereby,
Hear my clamorous complaint, though it late be,
Receive my prayers of thy benignity,
Though I be a sinner most abominable,
Yet let my name be written in Moses' table.
O Mary, pray to the Maker of all thing
Me for to help at my ending,
And save me from the power of my enemy;
For Death assaileth me strongly:
And, Lady, that I may by mean of thy prayer
Of your son's glory to be partiner.
By the mean of his passion I it crave;
I beseek you help me my soul to save.
Knowledge, give me the scourge of penance,
My flesh therewith shall give acquittance;
I will now begin, if God give me grace.

KNOWLEDGE.
Everyman, God give you time and space!
Thus I bequeath you in the hands of our Saviour;
Now may you make your reckoning sure.

EVERYMAN.
In the name of all the Holy Trinity,
My body punished sore shall be,
Take this body for the sin of the flesh;
Also thou delightest to go gay and fresh;
And in the way of damnation thou did me bring,
Therefore suffer now strokes and punishing:
Now of penance I will wade the water clear,
To save me from purgatory, that sharp fire.

GOOD DEEDS.
I thank God, now I can walk and go,
And am delivered of my sickness and woe;
Therefore with Everyman I will go, and not spare,
His good works I will help him to declare.

KNOWLEDGE.
Now, Everyman, be merry and glad;
Your Good Deeds cometh now, ye may not be sad:
Now is your Good Deeds whole and sound,
Going upright upon the ground.

EVERYMAN.
My heart is light, and shall be evermore;
Now will I smite faster than I did before.

GOOD DEEDS.
Everyman pilgrim, my special friend,
Blessed be thou without end;
For thee is prepared the eternal glory:
Ye have me made whole and sound,
Therefore I will bide by thee in every stound.[24]

EVERYMAN.
Welcome, my Good Deeds, now I hear thy voice,
I weep for very sweetness of love.

KNOWLEDGE.
Be no more sad, but evermore rejoice,
God seeth thy living in His throne above;
Put on this garment to thy behove,[25]
Which with your tears is now all wet,
Lest before God it be unsweet,
When ye to your journey's end come shall.

EVERYMAN.
Gentle Knowledge, what do ye it call?

KNOWLEDGE.
It is the garment of sorrow,
From pain it will you borrow;
Contrition it is,
That getteth forgiveness,
It pleaseth God passing-well.

GOOD DEEDS.
Everyman, will you wear it for your hele?[26]

EVERYMAN.
Now blessed be Jesu, Mary's son;
For now have I on true contrition:
And let us go now without tarrying.
Good Deeds, have we clear our reckoning?

GOOD DEEDS.
Yea, indeed, I have here.

EVERYMAN.
Then I trust we need not to fear;
Now, friends, let us not depart in twain.

KNOWLEDGE.
Nay, Everyman, that will we not certain.

GOOD DEEDS.
Yet must thou lead with thee
Three persons of great might.

EVERYMAN.
Who should they be?

GOOD DEEDS.
Discretion and Strength they hyght,[27]
And thy Beauty may not abide behind.

KNOWLEDGE.
Also ye must call to mind
Your Five Wits as for your councillors.

GOOD DEEDS.
You must have them ready at all hours.

EVERYMAN.
How shall I get them hither?

---

[24] time
[25] advantage

[26] health
[27] are called

KNOWLEDGE.
You must call them all together,
And they will hear you incontinent.[28]

EVERYMAN.
My friends, come hither, and be present,
Discretion, Strength, my Five Wits and Beauty.

BEAUTY.
Here at your will we be all ready;
What will ye that we should do?

GOOD DEEDS.
That ye would with Everyman go,
And help him in his pilgrimage:
Advise you, will ye go with him or not
    in that voyage?

STRENGTH.
We will bring him all thither
To help and comfort him, ye may believe me.

DISCRETION.
So will we go with him altogether.

EVERYMAN.
Almighty God, loved may Thou be;
I give Thee laud that I have hither brought
Strength, Discretion, Beauty, Five Wits:
    lack I nought:
And my Good Deeds, with Knowledge clear,
All be in my company at my will here;
I desire no more to my business.

STRENGTH.
And I Strength will by you stand in distress,
Though thou wouldest in battle
    fight on the ground.

FIVE WITS.
And though it were thorow[29] the world round,
We will not depart for sweet ne for sour.

BEAUTY.
No more will I unto death's hour,
Whatsoever thereof befall.

DISCRETION.
Everyman, advise you first of all,
Go with a good advisement and deliberation;
We all give you virtuous monition[30]
That all shall be well.

EVERYMAN.
My friends, hark what I will you tell;
I pray God reward you in His heavenly sphere:
Now hearken all that be here;
For I will make my testament
Here before you all present:
In alms half my good I will give
    with my hands twain
In the way of charity with good intent,
And the other half still shall remain:
I it bequeath to be returned there it ought to be.
This I do in despite of the fiend of hell,
To go quit[31] out of his peril
Ever after this day.

KNOWLEDGE.
Everyman, hearken what I will say;
Go to priesthood, I you advise,
And receive of him in any wise
The holy sacrament and ointment together,
Then shortly see ye turn again hither,
We will all abide you here.

FIVE WITS.
Yea, Everyman, hie you that ye ready were:
There is no emperor, king, duke, ne baron,

[29] through
[30] warning
[31] clear, free

_____
[28] without delay

66

That of God hath commission,
As hath the least priest in the world being;
For of the blessed sacraments pure and benign
He beareth the keys, and thereof hath cure
For man's redemption, it is ever sure,
Which God for our soul's medicine
Gave us out of his heart with great pain,
Here in this transitory life for thee and me:
The blessed sacraments seven there be,
Baptism, confirmation, with priesthood good,
And the sacrament of God's precious
    flesh and blood,
Marriage, the holy extreme unction, and penance;
These seven be good to have in remembrance,
Gracious sacraments of high divinity.

EVERYMAN.
Fain would I receive that holy body,
And meekly to my ghostly father I will go.

FIVE WITS.
Everyman, that is the best that ye can do;
God will you to salvation bring,
For good priesthood exceedeth all other thing;
To us holy scripture they do teach,
And converteth man from sin heaven to reach;

God hath to them more power given
Than to any angel that is in heaven:
With five words he may consecrate
God's body in flesh and blood to take,
And handleth his Maker between his hands,
The priest bindeth and unbindeth all bands
Both in earth and in heaven;
He ministers all the sacraments seven:
Though we kiss thy feet, thou wert worthy:
Thou art the surgeon that cureth sin deadly,
No remedy may we find under God,
But all only priesthood.
Everyman, God gave priests that dignity,
And setteth them in His stead among us to be;
Thus be they above angels in degree.

KNOWLEDGE.
If priests be good, it is so surely,
But when Jesu heng on the cross with great smart,
There he gave us out of his blessed heart
The same sacrament in great torment.
He sold them not to us, that Lord omnipotent;
Therefore Saint Peter the Apostle doth say,
That Jesus' curse hath all they,
Which God their Saviour do buy or sell,
Or they for any money do take or tell,
Sinful priests giveth the sinners example bad,
Their children sitteth by other men's fires,
    I have heard,
And some haunteth women's company,
With unclean life, as lusts of lechery;
These be with sin made blind.

FIVE WITS.
I trust to God, no such may we find:
Therefore let us priesthood honour,
And follow their doctrine for our soul's
    succour;
We be their sheep, and they shepherds be,
By whom we all be kept in surety.
Peace! for yonder I see Everyman come,
Which hath made true satisfaction.

GOOD DEEDS.
Methink it is he indeed.

EVERYMAN.
Now Jesu Christ be your alder speed!
I have received the sacrament for my redemption,
And then mine extreme unction;
Blessed be all they that counselled me to take it:
And now, friends, let us go without longer respite;
I thank God that ye have tarried so long.
Now set each of you on this rod your hand,
And shortly follow me;
I go before, there I would be:
God be our guide.

STRENGTH.
Everyman, we will not from you go,
Till ye have gone this voyage long.

DISCRETION.
I Discretion will bide by you also.

KNOWLEDGE.
And though this pilgrimage be never so strong,
I will never part you fro:
Everyman, I will be as sure by thee,
As ever I was by Judas Maccabee.

EVERYMAN.
Alas! I am so faint I may not stand,
My limbs under me do fold:
Friends, let us not turn again to this land,
Not for all the world's gold;
For into this cave must I creep,
And turn to the earth, and there to sleep.

BEAUTY.
What, into this grave? Alas!

EVERYMAN.
Yea, there shall ye consume³² more and less.

———————————
³² be consumed, decay

BEAUTY.
And what, should I smother here?

EVERYMAN.
Yea, by my faith, and never more appear;
In this world live no more we shall,
But in heaven before the highest Lord of all.

BEAUTY.
I cross out all this: adieu, by Saint John;
I take my cap in my lap, and am gone.

EVERYMAN.
What, Beauty? whither will ye?

BEAUTY.
Peace! I am deaf, I look not behind me,
Not, and thou wouldst give me
          all the gold in thy chest.

EVERYMAN.
Alas! whereto may I now trust?
Beauty doth fast away hie:
She promised with me to live and die.

STRENGTH.
Everyman, I will thee also forsake and deny,
The game liketh me not at all.

EVERYMAN.
Why then ye will forsake me all:
Strength, tarry, I pray you, a little space.

STRENGTH.
Nay, sir, by the rood³³ of grace,
I will hie me from thee fast,
Though thou weep till thy heart brast.³⁴

EVERYMAN.
Ye would ever bide by me, ye said.

———————————
³³ cross
³⁴ burst, break

68

STRENGTH.
Yea, I have you far enough conveyed:
Ye be old enough, I understand,
Your pilgrimage to take on hand;
I repent me, that I hither came.

EVERYMAN.
Strength, you to displease I am to blame;
Yet promise is debt; this ye well wot.

STRENGTH.
In faith, as for that I care not:
Thou art but a fool to complain;
Thou spendest thy speech and wasteth thy brain:
Go, thrist[35] thee into the ground.

EVERYMAN.
I had wend surer I should you have found:
But I see well, he that trusteth in his Strength,
Is greatly deceived at the length;
Both Strength and Beauty hath forsaken me,
Yet they promised me steadfast to be.

DISCRETION.
Everyman, I will after Strength be gone;
As for me, I will leave you alone.

EVERYMAN.
Why, Discretion, will ye forsake me?

DISCRETION.
Yea, in faith, I will go from thee;
For when Strength is gone before,
Then I follow after evermore.

EVERYMAN.
Yet, I pray thee, for love of the Trinity,
Look in my grave once piteously.

DISCRETION.
Nay, so nigh will I not come.
Now farewell, fellows everichone.[36]

EVERYMAN.
Oh, all thing faileth, save God alone,
Beauty, Strength, and Discretion;
For, when Death bloweth his blast,
They all run from me full fast.

FIVE WITS.
Everyman, of thee now my leave I take;
I will follow the other, for here I thee forsake.

EVERYMAN.
Alas! then may I both wail and weep;
For I took you for my best friend.

FIVE WITS.
I will no lenger thee keep:
Now farewell, and here an end.

EVERYMAN.
Now, Jesu, help! all hath forsaken me.

GOOD DEEDS.
Nay, Everyman, I will abide with thee,
I will not forsake thee indeed;
Thou shalt find me a good friend at need.

EVERYMAN.
Gramercy, Good Deeds, now may I
    true friends see
They have forsaken me everichone;
I loved them better than my good deeds alone:
Knowledge, will ye forsake me also?

---

[35] thrust

[36] every each one

KNOWLEDGE.
Yea, Everyman, when ye to death shall go;
But not yet for no manner of danger.

EVERYMAN.
Gramercy, Knowledge, with all my heart.

KNOWLEDGE.
Nay, yet I will not from hence depart,
Till I see where ye shall be come.

EVERYMAN.
Methinketh, alas! that I must be gone
To make my reckoning, and my debts pay;
For I see my time is nigh spent away.
Take ensample, all ye that this do hear or see,
How they that I loved best now forsake me;
Except my Good Deeds, that bideth truly.

GOOD DEEDS.
All earthly things is but vanity,
Beauty, Strength, and Discretion do man forsake,
Foolish friends and kinsmen, that fair spake;
All fleeth save Good Deeds, and that am I.

EVERYMAN.
Have mercy on me, God most mighty,
And stand by me, thou mother and maid Mary.

GOOD DEEDS.
Fear not, I will speak for thee.

EVERYMAN.
Here I cry, God mercy!

GOOD DEEDS.
Short our end and minish our pain:
Let us go, and never come again.

EVERYMAN.
Into thy hands, Lord, my soul I commend,
Receive it, Lord, that it be not lost;

As thou me boughtest, so me defend,
And save me from the fiend's boast,
That I may appear with that blessed host
That shall be saved at the day of doom:
In manus tuas,[37] of might most,
For ever *commendo spiritum meum.*[38]

            [*Everyman dies.*

KNOWLEDGE.
Now hath he suffered that we all shall endure:
The Good Deeds shall make all sure;
Now hath he made ending,
Methinketh that I hear angels sing,
And make great joy and melody,
Where Everyman's soul shall received be.

THE ANGEL.
Come, excellent elect spouse to Jesu,
Here above thou shalt go.
Because of thy singular virtue:
Now thy soul is taken thy body fro,
Thy reckoning is crystal clear;
Now shalt thou into the heavenly sphere,
Unto the which all ye shall come
That liveth well, after the day of doom.

---

[37] Into your hands
[38] I commend my spirit

DOCTOR.

This memory all men may have in mind;
Ye hearers, take it of worth, old and young,
And forsake pride, for he deceiveth you
    in the end,
And remember Beauty, Five Wits,
    Strength, and Discretion,
They all at last do Everyman forsake,
Save his Good Deeds; there doth he take:
But beware, for, and they be small,
Before God he hath no help at all;
None excuse may be there for Everyman:
Alas, how shall he do then?
For after death amends may no man make,
For then mercy and pity doth him forsake;

If his reckoning be not clear, when he doth come,
God will say, *"Ite, maledicti, in ignem
    aeternum"*;[39]
And he that hath his account whole and sound,
High in heaven he shall be crowned;
Unto which place God bring us all thither,
That we may live body and soul together;
Thereto help the Trinity:
Amen, say ye, for Saint Charity.

FINIS.

---

[39] Depart, cursed ones, into eternal fire

71

An Introduction to the Journal of Christopher Columbus From His First Voyage (1492)

Columbus provided his sponsors Ferdinand and Isabella with an account of his voyage.
According to his journal, Columbus kept two logs, a correct one for himself and a fudged one for the crew,
"that the crew might not be dismayed if the voyage should prove long."

In the Name of Our Lord Jesus Christ

Whereas, Most Christian, High, Excellent, and Powerful Princes, King and Queen of Spain and of the Islands of the Sea, our Sovereigns, this present year 1492, after your Highnesses had terminated the war with the Moors reigning in Europe, the same having been brought to an end in the great city of Granada, where on the second day of January, this present year, I saw the royal banners of your Highnesses planted by force of arms upon the towers of the Alhambra, which is the fortress of that city, and saw the Moorish king come out at the gate of the city and kiss the hands of your Highnesses, and of the Prince my Sovereign; and in the present month, in consequence of the information which I had given your Highnesses respecting the

Christopher Columbus

countries of India and of a Prince, called Great Can, which in our language signifies King of Kings, how, at many times he, and his predecessors had sent to Rome soliciting instructors who might teach him our holy faith, and the holy Father had never granted his request, whereby great numbers of people were lost, believing in idolatry and doctrines of perdition.

Your Highnesses, as Catholic Christians, and princes who love and promote the holy Christian faith, and are enemies of the doctrine of Mahomet, and of all idolatry and heresy, determined to send me, Christopher Columbus, to the above-mentioned countries of India, to see the said princes, people, and territories, and to learn their disposition and the proper method of converting them to our holy faith; and furthermore directed that I should not proceed by land to the East, as is customary, but by a Westerly route, in which direction we have hitherto no certain evidence that any one has gone. So after having expelled the Jews from your dominions, your Highnesses, in the same month of January, ordered me to proceed with a sufficient armament to the said regions of India, and for that purpose granted me great favors, and ennobled me that thenceforth I might call myself Don, and be High Admiral of the Sea, and perpetual Viceroy and Governor in all the islands and continents which I might discover and acquire, or which may hereafter be discovered and acquired in the ocean; and that this dignity should be inherited by my eldest son, and thus descend from degree to degree forever. Hereupon I left the city of Granada, on Saturday, the twelfth day of May, 1492, and proceeded to Palos, a seaport, where I armed three vessels, very fit for such an enterprise, and having provided myself with abundance of stores and seamen, I set sail from the port, on Friday, the third of August, half an hour before sunrise, and steered for the Canary Islands of your Highnesses which are in the said ocean, thence to take my departure and proceed till I arrived at the Indies, and perform the embassy of your Highnesses to the Princes there, and discharge the orders given me. For this purpose I determined to keep an account of the voyage, and to write down punctually every thing we performed or saw from day to day, as will hereafter appear.

Moreover, Sovereign Princes, besides describing every night the occurrences of the day, and every day those of the preceding night, I intend to draw up a nautical chart, which shall contain the several parts of the ocean and land in their proper situations; and also to compose a book to represent the whole by picture with latitudes and longitudes, on all which accounts it behooves me to abstain from my sleep, and make many trials in navigation, which things will demand much labor.

Excerpt from *The Praise of Folly* by Erasmus (1509)

On Popular Piety

Now what shall I say about those who find great comfort in soothing self-delusions about fictitious pardons [indulgences – grants of forgiveness from the church in exchange for donations made to the church; more will be said about these in the next unit] for their sins, measuring out the times in purgatory down to the droplets of a waterclock, parcelling out centuries, years, months, days, hours as if they were using mathematical tables? Or what about those who rely on certain little magical tokens and prayers thought up by some pious imposter for his own amusement or profit? They promise themselves anything and everything, perpetual health, a long life, flourishing old age, and finally a seat next to Christ among the saints, though this last they don't want

Erasmus

for quite a while yet – that is, when the pleasures of this life, to which they cling with all their might, have finally slipped through their fingers, then it will be soon enough to enter into the joys of the saints.

Imagine here, if you please, some merchant or soldier or judge who thinks that if he throws into the collection basket one coin from all his plunder, the whole cesspool of his sinful life will be immediately wiped out. He thinks all his acts of perjury, lust, drunkenness, quarreling, murder, deception, dishonesty, and betrayal are paid off like a mortgage, and paid off in such a way that he can start off once more on a whole new round of sinful pleasures. . .

And then too, isn't it pretty much the same sort of nonsense when particular regions lay claim to a certain saint, when they parcel out particular functions to particular saints, and assign to particular saints certain modes of worship: one offers relief from a toothache, another helps women in labor, another restores stolen goods; one shines as a ray of hope in a shipwreck, another takes care of the flocks – and so on with the others, for it would take far too long to list all of them. Some saints have a variety of powers, especially the virgin mother of God, to whom the ordinary run of men attribute more almost than to her son. . .

What a huge flock of people light candles to the virgin mother of God – even at noon, when there is no need! But how few of them strive to imitate her chastity, her modesty, her love for the things of heaven! For, in the last analysis, that is true worship, the kind which is by far the most pleasing to the saints in heaven . . .

Ninety-Five Theses
by Martin Luther (1517)

On the eve of All Saints Day, October 31, 1517, Martin Luther nailed a list of 95 theses or points for discussion on the front door of the Castle Church in Wittenberg. He denounced papal practices, including the selling of indulgences and the idea that the pope could forgive sins, as well as other doctrines and practices of the Catholic Church. He saw the trafficking in indulgences as only one symptom of a flawed system.

Martin Luther

Out of love for the truth and the desire to bring it to light, the following propositions will be discussed at Wittenberg, under the presidency of the Reverend Father Martin Luther, Master of Arts and of Sacred Theology, and Lecturer in Ordinary on the same at that place. Wherefore he requests that those who are unable to be present and debate orally with us, may do so by letter.

In the Name our Lord Jesus Christ. Amen.

1. Our Lord and Master Jesus Christ, when He said *Poenitentiam agite* [repent], willed that the whole life of believers should be repentance.

2. This word cannot be understood to mean sacramental penance, i.e., confession and satisfaction, which is administered by the priests.

3. Yet it means not inward repentance only; nay, there is no inward repentance which does not outwardly work divers mortifications of the flesh.

4. The penalty [of sin], therefore, continues so long as hatred of self continues; for this is the true inward repentance, and continues until our entrance into the kingdom of heaven.

5. The pope does not intend to remit, and cannot remit any penalties other than those which he has imposed either by his own authority or by that of the Canons.

6. The pope cannot remit any guilt, except by declaring that it has been remitted by God and by assenting to God's remission; though, to be sure, he may grant remission in cases reserved to his judgment. If his right to grant remission in such cases were despised, the guilt would remain entirely unforgiven.

7. God remits guilt to no one whom He does not, at the same time, humble in all things and bring into subjection to His vicar, the priest.

8. The penitential canons are imposed only on the living, and, according to them, nothing should be imposed on the dying.

9. Therefore the Holy Spirit in the pope is kind to us, because in his decrees he always makes exception of the article of death and of necessity.

10. Ignorant and wicked are the doings of those priests who, in the case of the dying, reserve canonical penances for purgatory.

11. This changing of the canonical penalty to the penalty of purgatory is quite evidently one of the tares that were sown while the bishops slept.

12. In former times the canonical penalties were imposed not after, but before absolution, as tests of true contrition.

13. The dying are freed by death from all penalties; they are already dead to canonical rules, and have a right to be released from them.

14. The imperfect health [of soul], that is to say, the imperfect love, of the dying brings with it, of necessity, great fear; and the smaller the love, the greater is the fear.

15. This fear and horror is sufficient of itself alone (to say nothing of other things) to constitute the penalty of purgatory, since it is very near to the horror of despair.

16. Hell, purgatory, and heaven seem to differ as do despair, almost-despair, and the assurance of safety.

17. With souls in purgatory it seems necessary that horror should grow less and love increase.

18. It seems unproved, either by reason or Scripture, that they are outside the state of merit, that is to say, of increasing love.

19. Again, it seems unproved that they, or at least that all of them, are certain or assured of their own blessedness, though we may be quite certain of it.

20. Therefore by "full remission of all penalties" the pope means not actually "of all," but only of those imposed by himself.

21. Therefore those preachers of indulgences are in error, who say that by the pope's indulgences a man is freed from every penalty, and saved;

22. Whereas he remits to souls in purgatory no penalty which, according to the canons, they would have had to pay in this life.

23. If it is at all possible to grant to any one the remission of all penalties whatsoever, it is certain that this remission can be granted only to the most perfect, that is, to the very fewest.

24. It must needs be, therefore, that the greater part of the people are deceived by that indiscriminate and highsounding promise of release from penalty.

25. The power which the pope has, in a general way, over purgatory, is just like the power which any bishop or curate has, in a special way, within his own diocese or parish.

26. The pope does well when he grants remission to souls [in purgatory], not by the power of the keys (which he does not possess), but by way of intercession.

27. They preach many who say that so soon as the penny jingles into the money-box, the soul flies out [of purgatory].

28. It is certain that when the penny jingles into the money-box, gain and avarice can be increased, but the result of the intercession of the Church is in the power of God alone.

29. Who knows whether all the souls in purgatory wish to be bought out of it, as in the legend of Sts. Severinus and Paschal.

30. No one is sure that his own contrition is sincere; much less that he has attained full remission.

31. Rare as is the man that is truly penitent, so rare is also the man who truly buys indulgences, i.e., such men are most rare.

32. They will be condemned eternally, together with their teachers, who believe themselves sure of their salvation because they have letters of pardon.

33. Men must be on their guard against those who say that the pope's pardons are that inestimable gift of God by which man is reconciled to Him;

34. For these "graces of pardon" concern only the penalties of sacramental satisfaction, and these are appointed by man.

35. They preach no Christian doctrine who teach that contrition is not necessary in those who intend to buy souls out of purgatory or to buy confessionalia.

36. Every truly repentant Christian has a right to full remission of penalty and guilt, even without letters of pardon.

37. Every true Christian, whether living or dead, has part in all the blessings of Christ and the Church; and this is granted him by God, even without letters of pardon.

38. Nevertheless, the remission and participation [in the blessings of the Church] which are granted by the pope are in no way to be despised, for they are, as I have said, the declaration of divine remission.

39. It is most difficult, even for the very keenest theologians, at one and the same time to commend to the people the abundance of pardons and [the need of] true contrition.

40. True contrition seeks and loves penalties, but liberal pardons only relax penalties and cause them to be hated, or at least, furnish an occasion [for hating them].

41. Apostolic pardons are to be preached with caution, lest the people may falsely think them preferable to other good works of love.

42. Christians are to be taught that the pope does not intend the buying of pardons to be compared in any way to works of mercy.

43. Christians are to be taught that he who gives to the poor or lends to the needy does a better work than buying pardons;

44. Because love grows by works of love, and man becomes better; but by pardons man does not grow better, only more free from penalty.

45. Christians are to be taught that he who sees a man in need, and passes him by, and gives [his money] for pardons, purchases not the indulgences of the pope, but the indignation of God.

46. Christians are to be taught that unless they have more than they need, they are bound to keep back what is necessary for their own families, and by no means to squander it on pardons.

47. Christians are to be taught that the buying of pardons is a matter of free will, and not of commandment.

48. Christians are to be taught that the pope, in granting pardons, needs, and therefore desires, their devout prayer for him more than the money they bring.

49. Christians are to be taught that the pope's pardons are useful, if they do not put their trust in them; but altogether harmful, if through them they lose their fear of God.

50. Christians are to be taught that if the pope knew the exactions of the pardon-preachers, he would rather that St. Peter's church should go to ashes, than that it should be built up with the skin, flesh and bones of his sheep.

51. Christians are to be taught that it would be the pope's wish, as it is his duty, to give of his own money to very many of those from whom certain hawkers of pardons cajole money, even though the church of St. Peter might have to be sold.

52. The assurance of salvation by letters of pardon is vain, even though the commissary, nay, even though the pope himself, were to stake his soul upon it.

53. They are enemies of Christ and of the pope, who bid the Word of God be altogether silent in some Churches, in order that pardons may be preached in others.

54. Injury is done the Word of God when, in the same sermon, an equal or a longer time is spent on pardons than on this Word.

55. It must be the intention of the pope that if pardons, which are a very small thing, are celebrated with one bell, with single processions and ceremonies, then the Gospel, which is the very greatest thing, should be preached with a hundred bells, a hundred processions, a hundred ceremonies.

56. The "treasures of the Church," out of which the pope grants indulgences, are not sufficiently named or known among the people of Christ.

57. That they are not temporal treasures is certainly evident, for many of the vendors do not pour out such treasures so easily, but only gather them.

58. Nor are they the merits of Christ and the Saints, for even without the pope, these always work grace for the inner man, and the cross, death, and hell for the outward man.

59. St. Lawrence said that the treasures of the Church were the Church's poor, but he spoke according to the usage of the word in his own time.

60. Without rashness we say that the keys of the Church, given by Christ's merit, are that treasure;

61. For it is clear that for the remission of penalties and of reserved cases, the power of the pope is of itself sufficient.

62. The true treasure of the Church is the Most Holy Gospel of the glory and the grace of God.

63. But this treasure is naturally most odious, for it makes the first to be last.

64. On the other hand, the treasure of indulgences is naturally most acceptable, for it makes the last to be first.

65. Therefore the treasures of the Gospel are nets with which they formerly were wont to fish for men of riches.

66. The treasures of the indulgences are nets with which they now fish for the riches of men.

67. The indulgences which the preachers cry as the "greatest graces" are known to be truly such, in so far as they promote gain.

68. Yet they are in truth the very smallest graces compared with the grace of God and the piety of the Cross.

69. Bishops and curates are bound to admit the commissaries of apostolic pardons, with all reverence.

70. But still more are they bound to strain all their eyes and attend with all their ears, lest these men preach their own dreams instead of the commission of the pope.

71. He who speaks against the truth of apostolic pardons, let him be anathema and accursed!

72. But he who guards against the lust and license of the pardon-preachers, let him be blessed!

73. The pope justly thunders against those who, by any art, contrive the injury of the traffic in pardons.

74. But much more does he intend to thunder against those who use the pretext of pardons to contrive the injury of holy love and truth.

75. To think the papal pardons so great that they could absolve a man even if he had committed an impossible sin and violated the Mother of God—this is madness.

76. We say, on the contrary, that the papal pardons are not able to remove the very least of venial sins, so far as its guilt is concerned.

77. It is said that even St. Peter, if he were now Pope, could not bestow greater graces; this is blasphemy against St. Peter and against the pope.

78. We say, on the contrary, that even the present pope, and any pope at all, has greater graces at his disposal; to wit, the Gospel, powers, gifts of healing, etc., as it is written in I Corinthians xii.

79. To say that the cross, emblazoned with the papal arms, which is set up [by the preachers of indulgences], is of equal worth with the Cross of Christ, is blasphemy.

80. The bishops, curates and theologians who allow such talk to be spread among the people, will have an account to render.

81. This unbridled preaching of pardons makes it no easy matter, even for learned men, to rescue the reverence due to the pope from slander, or even from the shrewd questionings of the laity.

82. To wit: – "Why does not the pope empty purgatory, for the sake of holy love and of the dire need of the souls that are there, if he redeems an infinite number of souls for the sake of miserable money with which to build a Church? The former reasons would be most just; the latter is most trivial."

83. Again: – "Why are mortuary and anniversary masses for the dead continued, and why does he not return or permit the withdrawal of the endowments founded on their behalf, since it is wrong to pray for the redeemed?"

84. Again: – "What is this new piety of God and the pope, that for money they allow a man who is impious and their enemy to buy out of purgatory the pious soul of a friend of God, and do not rather, because of that pious and beloved soul's own need, free it for pure love's sake?"

85. Again: – "Why are the penitential canons long since in actual fact and through disuse abrogated and dead, now satisfied by the granting of indulgences, as though they were still alive and in force?"

86. Again: – "Why does not the pope, whose wealth is to-day greater than the riches of the richest, build just this one church of St. Peter with his own money, rather than with the money of poor believers?"

87. Again: – "What is it that the pope remits, and what participation does he grant to those who, by perfect contrition, have a right to full remission and participation?"

88. Again: – "What greater blessing could come to the Church than if the pope were to do a hundred times a day what he now does once, and bestow on every believer these remissions and participations?"

89. "Since the pope, by his pardons, seeks the salvation of souls rather than money, why does he suspend the indulgences and pardons granted heretofore, since these have equal efficacy?"

90. To repress these arguments and scruples of the laity by force alone, and not to resolve them by giving reasons, is to expose the Church and the pope to the ridicule of their enemies, and to make Christians unhappy.

91. If, therefore, pardons were preached according to the spirit and mind of the pope, all these doubts would be readily resolved; nay, they would not exist.

92. Away, then, with all those prophets who say to the people of Christ, "Peace, peace," and there is no peace!

93. Blessed be all those prophets who say to the people of Christ, "Cross, cross," and there is no cross!

94. Christians are to be exhorted that they be diligent in following Christ, their Head, through penalties, deaths, and hell;

95. And thus be confident of entering into heaven rather through many tribulations, than through the assurance of peace.

Excerpts from Martin Luther's Speech Before the Diet of Worms (April 18, 1521)

Martin Luther was called to appear before church and civic officials at the Diet or Parliament in the city of Worms. This was a political body handling Luther's challenge to church authority because there was no line between church and state. Both institutions supported each other. There Luther gave a stirring defense of what he had done.

Most serene emperor, illustrious princes, gracious lords.

I obediently appeared at the time appointed yesterday evening, in conformity with the order given me yesterday, and by God's mercies I conjure your majesty and your august highnesses to listen graciously to the defense of a cause which I am assured is just and true. If, through ignorance, I should transgress the usages and proprieties of courts and should fail to give anyone the titles due to him or should act in some gestures or manner against courtly etiquette, I entreat you to pardon me; for I was not brought up in the palaces of kings, but in the seclusion of a cloister. I can say nothing of myself than that I have hitherto sought on earth through the simple-mindedness of my writings and teachings nothing but God's honour and the edification of believers.

Most serene Emperor, gracious electors, nobles and lords. Yesterday I was asked two questions: whether I would confess those pamphlets which were published under my name to be mine and whether I would persist in them or revoke them. To this I answered readily and clearly that I would now and for all eternity admit that these books were mine and were published under my name unless my opponents had changed them with deception or meddlesome wisdom or given false quotations. For I confess nothing but what I myself have written and certainly not the painstaking interpretations and comments of others.

Cathedral, Worms, Germany

Now I am called upon to answer the second question. I humbly pray your Imperial Majesty and lords, to consider carefully that my books are not all of the same kind. There are some in which I dealt with faith and life in such an evangelical and simple manner that even my opponents must admit that they are useful, innocent and worthy to be read by Christian people. Even the bull, which is otherwise quite fierce and cruel, considers some of my books quite harmless, though it condemns them on the basis of an unnatural judgment. Would I now revoke these books, I would do nothing but condemn the truth which is confessed by all, friend and foe alike. I of all men would be against a common and general confession.

The second group of books is written against the papacy and papal scheming and action, that is against those who through evil teaching and example have ruined Christendom, laying it waste with the evils of the spirit and the soul. No one can deny or obscure this fact, since experience and complaint of all men testify that the conscience of Christian believers is sneered at, harassed and tormented by the laws of the Pope and the doctrines of men. Likewise the goods and wealth of this most famous German nation were and are devoured through unbelievable tyranny in unreasonable manner, through decretals and laws, regulations and orders. Yet Canon Law states that the law and teaching of the Pope, whenever contrary to the Gospel and opinions of the holy Fathers, are to be considered in error and rejected. Were I, therefore, to revoke these books I would only strengthen this tyranny and open not only windows, but also doors for such unchristian ways, which would then flourish and rage more freely than ever before. The testimony of my opposition will make the rule of their bold and ignominious malice most intolerable for the poor suffering people.

The third group of my books consists of those I have written against certain private individuals who attempted to defend such Roman tyranny and denounce my pious doctrine. I confess that I have been more bitter and vehement against them than is in keeping with my Christian estate and calling. I do not claim to be a saint, nor do I proclaim my life, but rather the doctrine of Christ. Thus I cannot revoke these books, since my revocation would mean the continuance of their tyrannical, violent and raging rule due to my compliance and hesitancy. The people of God would be treated more violently and unmercifully than ever.

What more shall I say? Since I am a man and not God, I cannot support my pamphlets through any other means than that which the Lord Jesus employed when he was questioned before Ananias and asked concerning his teaching and smitten on his cheek by a servant. He said then: "If I have spoken evil bear witness of the evil." If the Lord, who knew that he could not err, did not refuse to hear testimony against his doctrine even from the most miserable servant, how much more should I, the scum of the earth and prone to error, hope and expect that someone should testify against my doctrine. Therefore I pray by the grace of God that your Imperial Majesty and Lordships, and everyone, high or low, should give such testimony, convict me of error and convince me with evangelical and prophetic writings. Should I thus be persuaded, I am most ready and willing to revoke all errors and be the first to throw my books into the fire.

From this it should be evident that I have carefully considered and weighed such discord, peril, uproar and rebellion which is rampant in the world today on account of my teaching, as I was gravely and urgently made aware yesterday. It is quite revealing as far as I am concerned that the divine word causes factions, misunderstanding, and discord to arise. Such, of course, must be the fate and the consequence of the divine Word, even as the Lord himself said: "I am come not to send peace but a sword, to set a son against his father, and a daughter against her mother, and the daughter in law against her mother in law. And a man's foes shall be they of his own household." Therefore we must ponder how wonderful and terrible God is in his counsels, plans and intentions. Perhaps we condemn the Word of God if we do away with our factions and dissensions. It could be a deluge of inestimable evils, indeed a cause of concern lest the imperial rule of our most pious and youthful Emperor should have an unfortunate beginning. . . .

Finally I commend myself to your Majesty and to your Lordships, humbly praying that you will not suffer me, against your will, to be subjected to disgrace and defamation by my enemies.

After this statement the spokesman for the Empire claimed angrily that I had not given a clear answer. Furthermore there was no need to discuss what has already been condemned and decided by councils. Therefore I was asked to answer in a simple and unsophisticated manner whether I would revoke. Thereupon I said: "Since your Imperial Majesty and Lordships demand a simple answer I will do so without horns or teeth as follows: Unless I am convicted by the testimony of Scripture or by evident reason—for I trust neither in popes nor in councils alone, since it is obvious that they have often erred and contradicted themselves—I am convicted by the Scripture which I have mentioned and my conscience is captive by the Word of God. Therefore I cannot and will not recant, since it is difficult, unprofitable and dangerous indeed to do anything against one's conscience. God help me. Amen."

1 Corinthians 13

Translated by William Tyndale (1525)

William Tyndale spent several years translating the New Testament and portions of the Old Testament from the original languages into English. His work has had tremendous influence on subsequent English translations.

Though I spake with the tonges of men and angels and yet had no love I were eve as soundinge brasse: or as a tynklynge Cymball. 2And though I coulde prophesy and vnderstode all secretes and all knowledge: yee yf I had all fayth so that I coulde move moutayns oute of ther places and yet had no love I were nothynge. 3And though I bestowed all my gooddes to fede ye poore and though I gave my body even that I burned and yet had no love it profeteth me nothinge. 4Love suffreth longe and is corteous. Love envieth not. Love doth not frowardly swelleth not dealeth 5not dishonestly seketh not her awne is not provoked to anger thynketh not evyll 6reioyseth not in iniquite: but reioyseth in ye trueth 7suffreth all thynge beleveth all thynges hopeth all thynges endureth in all thynges. 8Though that prophesyinge fayle other tonges shall cease or knowledge vanysshe awaye yet love falleth never awaye 9For oure knowledge is vnparfect and oure prophesyinge is vnperfet. 10But when yt which is parfect is come then yt which is vnparfet shall be done awaye. 11When I was a chylde I spake as a chylde I vnderstode as a childe I ymagened as a chylde. But assone as I was a man I put awaye childesshnes. 12Now we se in a glasse even in a darke speakynge: but then shall we se face to face. Now I knowe vnparfectly: but then shall I knowe even as I am knowen. 13Now abideth fayth hope and love even these thre: but the chefe of these is love.

A Mighty Fortress is Our God
by Martin Luther (1529)

*Martin Luther was a singer and played the lute. He wrote 35 hymns,
including this one that is often called the Battle Hymn of the Reformation.*

 mighty fortress is our God, a bulwark never failing;
Our helper He, amid the flood of mortal ills prevailing:
For still our ancient foe doth seek to work us woe;
His craft and power are great, and, armed with cruel hate,
On earth is not his equal.

Did we in our own strength confide, our striving would be losing;
Were not the right Man on our side, the Man of God's own choosing:
Dost ask who that may be? Christ Jesus, it is He;
Lord Sabaoth, His Name, from age to age the same,
And He must win the battle.

And though this world, with devils filled, should threaten to undo us,
We will not fear, for God hath willed His truth to triumph through us:
The Prince of Darkness grim, we tremble not for him;
His rage we can endure, for lo, his doom is sure,
One little word shall fell him.

That word above all earthly powers, no thanks to them, abideth;
The Spirit and the gifts are ours through Him Who with us sideth:
Let goods and kindred go, this mortal life also;
The body they may kill: God's truth abideth still,
His kingdom is forever.

Introduction to *Institutes of the Christian Religion* by John Calvin (1545)

John Calvin published the initial version of Institutes of the Christian Religion at age 26.
He revised it several times, with the final edition coming in 1559.
This preface was included in the French edition published at Geneva in 1545.

John Calvin

Subject of the Present Work

In order that my Readers may be the better able to profit by the present work, I am desirous briefly to point out the advantage which they may derive from it. For by so doing I will show them the end at which they ought to aim, and to which they ought to give their attention in reading it.

Although the Holy Scriptures contain a perfect doctrine, to which nothing can be added – our Lord having been pleased therein to unfold the infinite treasures of his wisdom – still every person, not intimately acquainted with them, stands in need of some guidance and direction, as to what he ought to look for in them, that he may not wander up and down, but pursue a certain path, and so attain the end to which the Holy Spirit invites him.

Hence it is the duty of those who have received from God more light than others to assist the simple in this matter, and, as it were, lend them their hand to guide and assist them in finding the sum of what God has been pleased to teach us in his word. Now, this cannot be better done in writing than by treating in succession of the principal matters which are comprised in Christian philosophy. For he who understands these will be prepared to make more progress in the school of God in one day than any other person in three months, inasmuch as he, in a great measure, knows to what he should refer each sentence, and has a rule by which to test whatever is presented to him.

Seeing, then, how necessary it was in this manner to aid those who desire to be instructed in the doctrine of salvation, I have endeavoured, according to the ability which God has given me, to employ myself in so doing, and with this view have composed the present book. And first I wrote it in Latin, that it might be serviceable to all studious persons, of what nation soever they might be; afterwards, desiring to communicate any fruit which might be in it to my French countrymen, I translated it into our own tongue. I dare not bear too strong a testimony in its favour, and declare how profitable the reading of it will be, lest I should seem to prize my own work too highly. However I may promise this much, that it will be a kind of key opening up to all the children of God a right and ready access to the understanding of the sacred volume. Wherefore, should our Lord give me henceforth means and opportunity of composing some Commentaries, I will use the greatest possible brevity, as there will be no occasion to make long digressions, seeing that I have in a manner deduced at length all the articles which pertain to Christianity.

And since we are bound to acknowledge that all truth and sound doctrine proceed from God, I will venture boldly to declare what I think of this work, acknowledging it to be God's work rather than mine. To him, indeed, the praise due to it must be ascribed. My opinion of the work then is this: I exhort all, who reverence the word of the Lord, to read it, and diligently imprint it on their memory, if they would, in the first place, have a summary of Christian doctrine, and, in the second place, an introduction to the profitable reading both of the Old and New Testament. When they shall have done so, they will know by experience that I have not wished to impose upon them with words. Should any one be unable to comprehend all that is contained in it, he must not, however, give it up in despair; but continue always to read on, hoping that one passage will give him a more familiar exposition of another. Above all things, I would recommend that recourse be had to Scripture in considering the proofs which I adduce from it.

Sonnet XVIII

by William Shakespeare (c. 1597)

In addition to his plays, William Shakespeare composed numerous sonnets.

Shall I compare thee to a summer's day?
Thou art more lovely and more temperate:
Rough winds do shake the darling buds of May,
And summer's lease hath all too short a date:
Sometime too hot the eye of heaven shines,
And often is his gold complexion dimm'd,
And every fair from fair sometime declines,
By chance, or nature's changing course untrimm'd:
But thy eternal summer shall not fade,
Nor lose possession of that fair thou ow'st,
Nor shall death brag thou wander'st in his shade,
When in eternal lines to time thou grow'st,
   So long as men can breathe, or eyes can see,
   So long lives this, and this gives life to thee.

William Shakespeare

Holy Sonnet 10 by John Donne (1633)

John Donne (1572-1631) led a varied life. He lived by the world's standards early on, then repented and became a respected Anglican minister. A collection of his poetry was published after his death. You will notice that many poets have given thought to the subject of death.

Death, be not proud, though some have callèd thee
Mighty and dreadful, for thou art not so;
For those whom thou think'st thou dost overthrow
Die not, poor death, nor yet canst thou kill me.
From rest and sleep, which yet thy pictures be,
Much pleasure, then from thee much more, must low
And soonest our best men with thee do go,
Rest of their bones and soul's delivery.
Thou art slave to fate, chance, kings and desperate men
And dost with poison, war and sickness dwell,
And poppy or charms can make us sleep as well
And better than thy stroke; why swell'st thou then?
One short sleep past, we wake eternally,
And death shall be no more; death, thou shalt die.

John Donne

On His Blindness by John Milton (1655)

John Milton (1608-1674) is considered by many to be the greatest English writer other than Shakespeare. His Paradise Lost *is an epic poem that takes the sin of Adam as its theme. He was a Puritan who served Oliver Cromwell. He also wrote the epic poems* Paradise Regained *and* Samson Agonistes *as well as other poems and essays. Apparently his arduous work for Cromwell brought on blindness, which is the subject of this poem.*

When I consider how my light is spent,
  E're half my days, in this dark world and wide,
  And that one Talent which is death to hide,
  Lodg'd with me useless, though my Soul more bent
To serve therewith my Maker, and present
  My true account, least he returning chide,
  Doth God exact day-labour, light deny'd,
  I fondly ask; But patience to prevent
That murmur, soon replies, God doth not need
  Either man's work or his own gifts, who best
  Bear his milde yoak, they serve him best, his State
Is Kingly. Thousands at his bidding speed
  And post o're Land and Ocean without rest:
  They also serve who only stand and waite.

John Milton's Cottage

John Milton and His Family

Awake, My Soul, and with the Sun
by Thomas Ken (1674)

When Thomas Ken wrote this song, the Church of England believed in singing Scripture only and that it was sinful to write new lyrics to be sung in church. The last verse is now known as the Doxology. He requested that it be sung at his funeral.

Awake, my soul, and with the sun
Thy daily stage of duty run;
Shake off dull sloth, and joyful rise,
To pay thy morning sacrifice.

Thy precious time misspent, redeem,
Each present day thy last esteem,
Improve thy talent with due care;
For the great day thyself prepare.

By influence of the Light divine
Let thy own light to others shine.
Reflect all Heaven's propitious ways
In ardent love, and cheerful praise.

In conversation be sincere;
Keep conscience as the noontide clear;
Think how all seeing God thy ways
And all thy secret thoughts surveys.

Wake, and lift up thyself, my heart,
And with the angels bear thy part,
Who all night long unwearied sing
High praise to the eternal King.

All praise to Thee, Who safe has kept
And hast refreshed me while I slept
Grant, Lord, when I from death shall wake
I may of endless light partake.

Heav'n is, dear Lord, where'er Thou art,
O never then from me depart;
For to my soul 'tis hell to be
But for one moment void of Thee.

Lord, I my vows to Thee renew;
Disperse my sins as morning dew.
Guard my first springs of thought and will,
And with Thyself my spirit fill.

Direct, control, suggest, this day,
All I design, or do, or say,
That all my powers, with all their might,
In Thy sole glory may unite.

Praise God, from Whom all blessings flow;
Praise Him, all creatures here below;
Praise Him above, ye heavenly host;
Praise Father, Son, and Holy Ghost.

Thomas Ken

Hymns by Isaac Watts (1674-1748)

Isaac Watts, like his father, was a Nonconformist or Dissenter. He wrote about 600 hymns during his life.
He finished school at age 20 and lived at home until he began his first teaching job at age 22.
He wrote many of his best hymns during those two years.

Am I a Soldier of the Cross?

Am I a soldier of the cross,
A follower of the Lamb,
And shall I fear to own His cause,
Or blush to speak His Name?

Must I be carried to the skies
On flowery beds of ease,
While others fought to win the prize,
And sailed through bloody seas?

Are there no foes for me to face?
Must I not stem the flood?
Is this vile world a friend to grace,
To help me on to God?

Sure I must fight if I would reign;
Increase my courage, Lord.
I'll bear the toil, endure the pain,
Supported by Thy Word.

Thy saints in all this glorious war
Shall conquer, though they die;
They see the triumph from afar,
By faith's discerning eye.

When that illustrious day shall rise,
And all Thy armies shine
In robes of victory through skies,
The glory shall be Thine.

Joy to the World

Joy to the world, the Lord is come!
Let earth receive her King;
Let every heart prepare Him room,
And heaven and nature sing,
And heaven and nature sing,
And heaven, and heaven,
    and nature sing.

Joy to the world, the Savior reigns!
Let men their songs employ;
While fields and floods,
    rocks, hills and plains
Repeat the sounding joy,
Repeat the sounding joy,
Repeat, repeat, the sounding joy.

No more let sins and sorrows grow,
Nor thorns infest the ground;
He comes to make His blessings flow
Far as the curse is found,
Far as the curse is found,
Far as, far as, the curse is found.

He rules the world with
    truth and grace,
And makes the nations prove
The glories of His righteousness,
And wonders of His love,
And wonders of His love,
And wonders, wonders, of His love.

How Shall the Young Secure Their Hearts?

How shall the young secure their hearts
And guard their lives from sin?
Thy Word the choicest rules imparts
To keep the conscience clean.

When once it enters to the mind,
It spreads such light abroad,
The meanest souls instruction find,
And raise their thoughts to God.

'Tis, like the sun, a heav'nly light
That guides us all the day,
And through the dangers of the night
A lamp to lead our way.

The men that keep Thy law with care,
And meditate Thy Word,
Grow wiser than their teachers are,
And better know the Lord.

Thy precepts make me truly wise:
I hate the sinner's road;
I hate my own vain thoughts that rise,
But love Thy law, my God.

The starry heav'ns Thy rule obey,
The earth maintains her place;
And these Thy servants, night and day,
Thy skill and power express.

But still Thy law and Gospel, Lord,
Have lessons more divine;
Not earth stands firmer than Thy Word,
Nor stars so nobly shine.

Thy Word is everlasting truth;
How pure is every page!
That holy Book shall guide our youth
And well support our age.

I'm Not Ashamed to Own My Lord

I'm not ashamed to own my Lord,
Or to defend His cause;
Maintain the honor of His Word,
The glory of His cross.

Jesus, my God! I know His Name,
His Name is all my trust;
Nor will He put my soul to shame,
Nor let my hope be lost.

Firm as His throne His promise stands,
And He can well secure
What I've committed to His hands
Till the decisive hour.

Then will He own my worthless name
Before His Father's face,
And in the new Jerusalem
Appoint my soul a place.

Isaac Watts

93

Come, Holy Spirit, Heavenly Dove

Come, Holy Spirit, heavenly Dove,
With all Thy quick'ning powers;
Kindle a flame of sacred love
In these cold hearts of ours.

Look how we grovel here below,
Fond of these trifling toys;
Our souls can neither fly nor go
To reach eternal joys.

In vain we tune our formal songs,
In vain we strive to rise;
Hosannas languish on our tongues,
And our devotion dies.

Dear Lord! and shall we ever live
At this poor dying rate?
Our love so faint, so cold to Thee,
And Thine to us so great!

Come, Holy Spirit, heavenly Dove,
With all Thy quick'ning powers;
Come, shed abroad the Savior's love
And that shall kindle ours.

When I Survey the Wondrous Cross

When I survey the wondrous cross
On which the Prince of glory died,
My richest gain I count but loss,
And pour contempt on all my pride.

Forbid it, Lord, that I should boast,
Save in the death of Christ my God!
All the vain things that charm me most,
I sacrifice them to His blood.

See from His head, His hands, His feet,
Sorrow and love flow mingled down!
Did e'er such love and sorrow meet,
Or thorns compose so rich a crown?

His dying crimson, like a robe,
Spreads o'er His body on the tree;
Then I am dead to all the globe,
And all the globe is dead to me.

Were the whole realm of nature mine,
That were a present far too small;
Love so amazing, so divine,
Demands my soul, my life, my all.

Preface to *Philosophiae Naturalis Principia Mathematica* by Isaac Newton (1686)

Since the ancients (as we are told by Pappus) made great account of the science of mechanics in the investigation of natural things; and the moderns, laying aside substantial forms and occult qualities, have endeavored to subject the phenomena of nature to the laws of mathematics, I have in this treatise cultivated mathematics so far as it regards philosophy. The ancients considered mechanics in a twofold respect; as rational, which proceeds accurately by demonstration, and practical. To practical mechanics all the manual arts belong, from which mechanics took its name.

Isaac Newton

But as artificers do not work with perfect accuracy, it comes to pass that mechanics is so distinguished from geometry, that what is perfectly accurate is called geometrical; what is less so is called mechanical. But the errors are not in the art, but in the artificers. He that works with less accuracy is an imperfect mechanic: and if any could work with perfect accuracy, he would be the most perfect mechanic of all; for the description of right lines and circles, upon which geometry is founded, belongs to mechanics.

Geometry does not teach us to draw these lines, but requires them to be drawn; for it requires that the learner should first be taught to describe these accurately, before he enters upon geometry; then it shows how by these operations problems may be solved. To describe right lines and circles are problems, but not geometrical problems. The solution of these problems is required from mechanics; and by geometry the use of them, when so solved, is shown; and it is the glory of geometry that from those few principles, fetched from without, it is able to produce so many things.

Therefore geometry is founded in mechanical practice, and is nothing but that part of universal mechanics which accurately proposes and demonstrates the art of measuring. But since the manual arts are chiefly conversant in the moving of bodies, it comes to pass that geometry is commonly referred to their magnitudes, and mechanics to their motion. In this sense rational mechanics will be the science of motions resulting from any forces whatsoever, and of the forces required to produce any motions, accurately proposed and demonstrated. This part of mechanics was cultivated by the ancients in the five powers which relate to manual arts, who considered gravity (it not being a manual power) no otherwise than as it moved weights by those powers.

Our design, not respecting arts, but philosophy, and our subject, not manual, but natural powers, we consider chiefly those things which relate to gravity, levity, elastic force, the resistance of fluids, and the like forces, whether attractive or impulsive; and therefore we offer this work as mathematical principles of philosophy; for all the difficulty of philosophy seems to consist in this—from the phenomena of motions to investigate the forces of nature, and then from these forces to demonstrate the other phenomena; and to this end the general propositions in the first and second book are directed. In the third book we give an example of this in the explication of the system of the World; for by the propositions mathematically demonstrated in the first book, we there derive from the celestial phenomena the forces of gravity with which bodies tend to the sun and the several planets.

Then, from these forces, by other propositions which are also mathematical, we deduce the motions of the planets, the comets, the moon, and the sea. I wish we could derive the rest of the phenomena of nature by the same kind of reasoning from mechanical principles; for I am induced by many reasons to suspect that they may all depend upon certain forces by which the particles of bodies, by some causes hitherto unknown, are either mutually impelled towards each other, and cohere in regular figures, or are repelled and recede from each other; which forces being unknown, philosophers have hitherto attempted the search of nature in vain; but I hope the principles here laid down will afford some light either to that or some truer method of philosophy.

In the publication of this work, the most acute and universally learned Mr. Edmund Halley not only assisted me with his pains in correcting the press and taking care of the schemes, but it was to his solicitations that its becoming public is owing; for when he had obtained of me my demonstrations of the figure of the celestial orbits, he continually pressed me to communicate the same to the Royal Society, who afterwards, by their kind encouragement and entreaties, engaged me to think of publishing them. But after I had begun to consider the inequalities of the lunar motions, and had entered upon some other things relating to the laws and measures of gravity, and other forces; and the figures that would be described by bodies attracted according to given laws; and the motion of several bodies moving among themselves; the motion of bodies in resisting mediums; the forces, densities, and motions of mediums; the orbits of the comets, and such like; I put off that publication till I had made a search into those matters, and could put out the whole together.

What relates to the lunar motions (being imperfect) I have put all together in the corollaries of proposition 66, to avoid being obliged to propose and distinctly demonstrate the several things there contained in a method more prolix than the subject deserved, and interrupt the series of the several propositions. Some things, found out after the rest, I chose to insert in places less suitable, rather than change the number of the propositions and the citations. I heartily beg that what I have here done may be read with candor; and that the defects I have been guilty of upon this difficult subject may be not so much reprehended as kindly supplied, and investigated by new endeavors of my readers.

Isaac Newton
Cambridge, Trinity College,
May 8, 1686

Excerpts from the English Bill of Rights (1689)

When the Catholic King James II fled from England, Parliament declared that he had abdicated and offered the throne to William and Mary. The next year, the new monarchs signed a Bill of Rights, guaranteeing certain protections to individuals and insuring that a Catholic could not assume the throne.

Mary and William

[. . . Parliament hereby declares:]

That the pretended power of suspending the laws or the execution of laws by regal authority without consent of Parliament is illegal;

That the pretended power of dispensing with laws or the execution of laws by regal authority, as it hath been assumed and exercised of late, is illegal;

That the commission for erecting the late Court of Commissioners for Ecclesiastical Causes, and all other commissions and courts of like nature, are illegal and pernicious;

That levying money for or to the use of the Crown by pretence of prerogative, without grant of Parliament, for longer time, or in other manner than the same is or shall be granted, is illegal;

That it is the right of the subjects to petition the king, and all commitments and prosecutions for such petitioning are illegal;

That the raising or keeping a standing army within the kingdom in time of peace, unless it be with consent of Parliament, is against law;

That the subjects which are Protestants may have arms for their defence suitable to their conditions and as allowed by law;

That election of members of Parliament ought to be free;

That the freedom of speech and debates or proceedings in Parliament ought not to be impeached or questioned in any court or place out of Parliament;

That excessive bail ought not to be required, nor excessive fines imposed, nor cruel and unusual punishments inflicted;

That jurors ought to be duly impanelled and returned, and jurors which pass upon men in trials for high treason ought to be freeholders;

That all grants and promises of fines and forfeitures of particular persons before conviction are illegal and void;

And that for redress of all grievances, and for the amending, strengthening and preserving of the laws, Parliaments ought to be held frequently.

. . .

And whereas it hath been found by experience that it is inconsistent with the safety and welfare of this Protestant kingdom to be governed by a popish prince, or by any king or queen marrying a papist, the said Lords Spiritual and Temporal and Commons do further pray that it may be enacted, that all and every person and persons that is, are or shall be reconciled to or shall hold communion with the see or Church of Rome, or shall profess the popish religion, or shall marry a papist, shall be excluded and be for ever incapable to inherit, possess or enjoy the crown and government of this realm and Ireland and the dominions thereunto belonging or any part of the same, or to have, use or exercise any regal power, authority or jurisdiction within the same. . . .

Well-Dressed
English Man 1670

Well-Dressed
English Woman 1670

Excerpt from Book Two of
Two Treatises of Government
by John Locke (1690)

CHAP. IX. Of the Ends of Political Society and Government.

Sec. 123. IF man in the state of nature be so free, as has been said; if he be absolute lord of his own person and possessions, equal to the greatest, and subject to no body, why will he part with his freedom? why will he give up this empire, and subject himself to the dominion and controul of any other power? To which it is obvious to answer, that though in the state of nature he hath such a right, yet the enjoyment of it is very uncertain, and  constantly exposed to the invasion of others: for all being kings as much as he, every man his equal, and the greater part no strict observers of equity and justice, the enjoyment of the property he has in this state is very unsafe, very unsecure. This makes him willing to quit a condition, which, however free, is full of fears and continual dangers: and it is not without reason, that he seeks out, and is willing to join in society with others, who are already united, or have a mind to unite, for the mutual preservation of their lives, liberties and estates, which I call by the general name, property.

Sec. 124. The great and chief end, therefore, of men's uniting into commonwealths, and putting themselves under government, is the preservation of their property. To which in the state of nature there are many things wanting. First, there wants an established, settled, known law, received and allowed by common consent to be the standard of right and wrong, and the common measure to decide all controversies between them: for though the law of nature be plain and intelligible to all rational creatures; yet men being biased by their interest, as well as ignorant for want of study of it, are not apt to allow of it as a law binding to them in the application of it to their particular cases.

Sec. 125. Secondly, in the state of nature there wants a known and indifferent judge, with authority to determine all differences according to the established law: for every one in that state being both judge and executioner of the law of nature, men being partial to themselves, passion and revenge is very apt to carry them too far, and with too much heat, in their own cases; as well as negligence, and unconcernedness, to make them too remiss in other men's.

Sec. 126. Thirdly, in the state of nature there often wants power to back and support the sentence when right, and to give it due execution. They who by any injustice offended, will seldom fail, where they are able, by force to make good their injustice; such resistance many times makes the punishment dangerous, and frequently destructive, to those who attempt it.

Sec. 127. Thus mankind, notwithstanding all the privileges of the state of nature, being but in an ill condition, while they remain in it, are quickly driven into society. Hence it comes to pass, that we seldom find any number of men live any time together in this state. The inconveniencies that they are therein exposed to, by the irregular and uncertain exercise of the power every man has of punishing the transgressions of others, make them take sanctuary under the established laws of government, and therein seek the preservation of their property. It is this makes them so willingly give up every one his single power of punishing, to be exercised by such alone, as shall be appointed to it amongst them; and by such rules as the community, or those authorized by them to that purpose, shall agree on. And in this we have the original right and rise of both the legislative and executive power, as well as of the governments and societies themselves.

Sec. 128. For in the state of nature, to omit the liberty he has of innocent delights, a man has two powers. The first is to do whatsoever he thinks fit for the preservation of himself, and others within the permission of the law of nature: by which law, common to them all, he and all the rest of mankind are one community, make up one society, distinct from all other creatures. And were it not for the corruption and vitiousness of degenerate men, there would be no need of any other; no necessity that men should separate from this great and natural community, and by positive agreements combine into smaller and divided associations. The other power a man has in the state of nature, is the power to punish the crimes committed against that law. Both these he gives up, when he joins in a private, if I may so call it, or particular politic society, and incorporates into any common-wealth, separate from the rest of mankind.

Sec. 129. The first power, viz. of doing whatsoever he thought for the preservation of himself, and the rest of mankind, he gives up to be regulated by laws made by the society, so far forth as the preservation of himself, and the rest of that society shall require; which laws of the society in many things confine the liberty he had by the law of nature.

Sec. 130. Secondly, the power of punishing he wholly gives up, and engages his natural force, (which he might before employ in the execution of the law of nature, by his own single authority, as he thought fit) to assist the executive power of the society, as the law thereof shall require: for being now in a new state, wherein he is to enjoy many conveniencies, from the labour, assistance, and society of others in the same community, as well as protection from its whole strength; he is to part also with as much of his natural liberty, in providing for himself, as the good, prosperity, and safety of the society shall require; which is not only necessary, but just, since the other members of the society do the like.

Sec. 131.   But though men, when they enter into society, give up the equality, liberty, and executive power they had in the state of nature, into the hands of the society, to be so far disposed of by the legislative, as the good of the society shall require; yet it being only with an intention in every one the better to preserve himself, his liberty and property; (for no rational creature can be supposed to change his condition with an intention to be worse) the power of the society, or legislative constituted by them, can never be supposed to extend farther, than the common good; but is obliged to secure every one's property, by providing against those three defects above mentioned, that made the state of nature so unsafe and uneasy. And so whoever has the legislative or supreme power of any common-wealth, is bound to govern by established standing laws, promulgated and known to the people, and not by extemporary decrees; by indifferent and upright judges, who are to decide controversies by those laws; and to employ the force of the community at home, only in the execution of such laws, or abroad to prevent or redress foreign injuries, and secure the community from inroads and invasion. And all this to be directed to no other end, but the peace, safety, and public good of the people.

The Spacious Firmament on High
by Joseph Addison (1712)

The essayist Joseph Addison contributed regular pieces for the English journal The Spectator.
In 1712, he wrote an essay on the best way to strengthen and confirm faith in God.
The piece concluded with this "Ode," an interpretation of Psalm 19 which was set to music written by
Franz Joseph Haydn in 1798. It is now known as the hymn, "The Spacious Firmament on High."
(Note: In the first stanza, Original means Originator or Creator)

The spacious firmament on high,
With all the blue ethereal sky,
And spangled heavens, a shining frame
Their great Original proclaim.
Th' unwearied sun, from day to day,
Does his Creator's power display,
And publishes to every land
The work of an Almighty Hand.

Soon as the evening shades prevail
The moon takes up the wondrous tale,
And nightly to the listening earth
Repeats the story of her birth;
While all the stars that round her burn
And all the planets in their turn,
Confirm the tidings as they roll,
And spread the truth from pole to pole.

What though in solemn silence all
Move round the dark terrestrial ball?
What though no real voice nor sound
Amid the radiant orbs be found?
In reason's ear they all rejoice,
And utter forth a glorious voice,
Forever singing as they shine,
"The hand that made us is divine."

Joseph Addison (1672-1719)

God Moves in a Mysterious Way
by William Cowper (1774)

Son of a chaplain to King George II, Cowper (pronounced "Cooper"),
co-wrote the Olney Hymns with John Newton, author of "Amazing Grace."

God moves in a mysterious way
His wonders to perform;
He plants His footsteps in the sea
And rides upon the storm.

Deep in unfathomable mines
Of never failing skill
He treasures up His bright designs
And works His sovereign will.

Ye fearful saints, fresh courage take;
The clouds ye so much dread
Are big with mercy and shall break
In blessings on your head.

William Cowper

Judge not the Lord by feeble sense,
But trust Him for His grace;
Behind a frowning providence
He hides a smiling face.

His purposes will ripen fast,
Unfolding every hour;
The bud may have a bitter taste,
But sweet will be the flower.

Blind unbelief is sure to err
And scan His work in vain;
God is His own interpreter,
And He will make it plain.

Hymns by Charles Wesley
(1707-1788)

Charles Wesley wrote over 6,000 hymns. Charles and his brother John founded the Methodist movement.

Love Divine, All Loves Excelling

Love divine, all loves excelling,
Joy of heaven to earth come down;
Fix in us thy humble dwelling;
All thy faithful mercies crown!
Jesus, Thou art all compassion,
Pure unbounded love Thou art;
Visit us with Thy salvation;
Enter every trembling heart.

Breathe, O breathe Thy loving Spirit,
Into every troubled breast!
Let us all in Thee inherit;
Let us find that second rest.
Take away our bent to sinning;
Alpha and Omega be;
End of faith, as its Beginning,
Set our hearts at liberty.

Come, Almighty to deliver,
Let us all Thy life receive;
Suddenly return and never,
Never more Thy temples leave.
Thee we would be always blessing,
Serve Thee as Thy hosts above,
Pray and praise Thee without ceasing,
Glory in Thy perfect love.

Finish, then, Thy new creation;
Pure and spotless let us be.
Let us see Thy great salvation
Perfectly restored in Thee;
Changed from glory into glory,
Till in heaven we take our place,
Till we cast our crowns before Thee,
Lost in wonder, love, and praise.

A Charge to Keep I Have

A charge to keep I have,
A God to glorify,
A never-dying soul to save,
And fit it for the sky.

To serve the present age,
My calling to fulfill:
O may it all my powers engage
To do my Master's will!

Arm me with jealous care,
As in Thy sight to live;
And O Thy servant, Lord, prepare
A strict account to give!

Help me to watch and pray,
And on Thyself rely,
Assured, if I my trust betray,
I shall for ever die.

Jesus, Lover of My Soul

Jesus, lover of my soul, let me to Thy bosom fly,
While the nearer waters roll, while the tempest still is high.
Hide me, O my Savior, hide, till the storm of life is past;
Safe into the haven guide; O receive my soul at last.

Other refuge have I none, hangs my helpless soul on Thee;
Leave, ah! leave me not alone, still support and comfort me.
All my trust on Thee is stayed, all my help from Thee I bring;
Cover my defenseless head with the shadow of Thy wing.

Wilt Thou not regard my call? Wilt Thou not accept my prayer?
Lo! I sink, I faint, I fall—Lo! on Thee I cast my care;
Reach me out Thy gracious hand! While I of Thy strength receive,
Hoping against hope I stand, dying, and behold, I live.

Thou, O Christ, art all I want, more than all in Thee I find;
Raise the fallen, cheer the faint, heal the sick, and lead the blind.
Just and holy is Thy Name, I am all unrighteousness;
False and full of sin I am; Thou art full of truth and grace.

Plenteous grace with Thee is found, grace to cover all my sin;
Let the healing streams abound; make and keep me pure within.
Thou of life the fountain art, freely let me take of Thee;
Spring Thou up within my heart; rise to all eternity.

Christ, the Lord, is Risen Today

Christ, the Lord, is risen today, Alleluia!
Sons of men and angels say, Alleluia!
Raise your joys and triumphs high, Alleluia!
Sing, ye heavens, and earth, reply, Alleluia!

Love's redeeming work is done, Alleluia!
Fought the fight, the battle won, Alleluia!
Lo! the Sun's eclipse is over, Alleluia!
Lo! He sets in blood no more, Alleluia!

Vain the stone, the watch, the seal, Alleluia!
Christ hath burst the gates of hell, Alleluia!
Death in vain forbids His rise, Alleluia!
Christ hath opened paradise, Alleluia!

Lives again our glorious King, Alleluia!
Where, O death, is now thy sting? Alleluia!
Once He died our souls to save, Alleluia!
Where thy victory, O grave? Alleluia!

Soar we now where Christ hath led, Alleluia!
Following our exalted Head, Alleluia!
Made like Him, like Him we rise, Alleluia!
Ours the cross, the grave, the skies, Alleluia!

Hail, the Lord of earth and heaven, Alleluia!
Praise to Thee by both be given, Alleluia!
Thee we greet triumphant now, Alleluia!
Hail, the resurrection day, Alleluia!

King of glory, Soul of bliss, Alleluia!
Everlasting life is this, Alleluia!
Thee to know, Thy power to prove, Alleluia!
Thus to sing and thus to love, Alleluia!

Come, Thou Almighty King

Come, Thou almighty King,
Help us Thy Name to sing, help us to praise!
Father all glorious, over all victorious,
Come and reign over us, Ancient of Days!

Jesus, our Lord, arise,
Scatter our enemies, and make them fall;
Let Thine almighty aid our sure defense be
    made,
Souls on Thee be stayed; Lord, hear our call.

Come, Thou incarnate Word,
Gird on Thy mighty sword,
    our prayer attend!
Come, and Thy people bless, and give Thy
    Word success,
Spirit of holiness, on us descend!

Come, holy Comforter,
Thy sacred witness bear in this glad hour.
Thou Who almighty art, now rule in every
    heart,
And ne'er from us depart, Spirit of power!

To Thee, great One in Three,
Eternal praises be, hence, evermore.
Thy sovereign majesty may we in glory see,
And to eternity love and adore!

Charles Wesley

106

On the Death of a Favourite Cat, Drowned in a China Tub of Gold Fishes by Thomas Gray (1742)

Thomas Gray (1716-1771) was a forerunner of the Romantic poets. The following two poems reflect two different moods: one humorous and one somber. The "Elegy" made Gray an immediate success as a poet.

'Twas on a lofty vase's side,
  Where China's gayest art had dyed
    The azure flowers that blow,
  Demurest of the tabby kind,
  The pensive Selima, reclined,
    Gazed on the lake below.

Her conscious tail her joy declared;
  The fair round face, the snowy beard,
    The velvet of her paws,
  Her coat that with the tortoise vies,
  Her ears of jet, and emerald eyes,
    She saw, and purr'd applause.

Still had she gazed, but, 'midst the tide,
  Two angel forms were seen to glide,
    The Genii of the stream;
  Their scaly armour's Tyrian hue,
  Through richest purple, to the view
    Betray'd a golden gleam.

The hapless nymph with wonder saw;
  A whisker first, and then a claw,
    With many an ardent wish,
  She stretch'd in vain to reach the prize:
  What female heart can gold despise?
    What cat's averse to fish?

Presumptuous maid! with looks intent,
  Again she stretch'd, again she bent,
    Nor knew the gulf between:
  (Maligant Fate sat by and smiled,)
  The slippery verge her feet beguiled;
    She tumbled headlong in.

Eight times emerging from the flood,
  She mew'd to every watery god
    Some speedy aid to send.
  No Dolphin came, no Nereid stirr'd,
  Nor cruel Tom or Susan heard:
    A favourite has no friend!

From hence, ye beauties! undeceived,
  Know one false step is ne'er retrieved,
    And be with caution bold:
  Not all that tempts your wandering eyes,
  And heedless hearts, is lawful prize,
    Nor all that glisters gold.

Elegy Written in a Country Churchyard
by Thomas Gray (1751)

The curfew tolls the knell of parting day,
    The lowing herd wind slowly o'er the lea,
The ploughman homeward plods his weary way,
    And leaves the world to darkness and to me.

Now fades the glimmering landscape on the sight,
    And all the air a solemn stillness holds,
Save where the beetle wheels his droning flight,
    And drowsy tinklings lull the distant folds:

Save that, from yonder ivy-mantled tower,
    The moping owl does to the moon complain
Of such as, wandering near her secret bower,
    Molest her ancient solitary reign.

Beneath those rugged elms, that yew-tree's shade,
    Where heaves the turf in many a mouldering heap,
Each in his narrow cell for ever laid,
    The rude forefathers of the hamlet sleep.

The breezy call of incense-breathing Morn,
    The swallow twittering from the straw-built shed,
The cock's shrill clarion, or the echoing horn,
    No more shall rouse them from their lowly bed.

For them no more the blazing hearth shall burn,
    Or busy housewife ply her evening care;
No children run to lisp their sire's return,
    Or climb his knees, the envied kiss to share.

Oft did the harvest to their sickle yield,
    Their furrow oft the stubborn glebe has broke;
How jocund did they drive their team afield!
    How bow'd the woods beneath their sturdy stroke!

Let not Ambition mock their useful toil,
    Their homely joys, and destiny obscure;
Nor Grandeur hear with a disdainful smile
    The short and simple annals of the poor.

The boast of heraldry, the pomp of power,
    And all that beauty, all that wealth e'er gave,
Await alike the inevitable hour:
    The paths of glory lead but to the grave.

Nor you, ye Proud! impute to these the fault,
    If Memory o'er their tomb no trophies raise,
Where, through the long-drawn aisle and fretted vault,
    The pealing anthem swells the note of praise.

Can storied urn or animated bust
    Back to its mansion call the fleeting breath?
Can Honour's voice provoke the silent dust,
    Or Flattery soothe the dull cold ear of death?

Perhaps in this neglected spot is laid
    Some heart once pregnant with celestial fire;
Hands that the rod of empire might have sway'd,
    Or waked to ecstasy the living lyre.

But Knowledge to their eyes her ample page,
    Rich with the spoils of Time, did ne'er unroll;
Chill Penury repress'd their noble rage,
    And froze the genial current of the soul.

Full many a gem of purest ray serene
    The dark unfathom'd caves of ocean bear:
Full many a flower is born to blush unseen,
    And waste its sweetness on the desert air.

Some village Hampden, that with dauntless breast
    The little tyrant of his fields withstood,
Some mute inglorious Milton here may rest,
    Some Cromwell, guiltless of his country's blood.

The applause of listening senates to command,
    The threats of pain and ruin to despise,
To scatter plenty o'er a smiling land,
    And read their history in a nation's eyes,

Their lot forbade; nor circumscribed alone
    Their growing virtues, but their crimes confined;
Forbade to wade through slaughter to a throne,
    And shut the gates of Mercy on mankind,

The struggling pangs of conscious Truth to hide,
    To quench the blushes of ingenuous Shame,
Or heap the shrine of Luxury and Pride
    With incense kindled at the Muse's flame.

Far from the madding crowd's ignoble strife,
    Their sober wishes never learn'd to stray;
Along the cool sequester'd vale of life
    They kept the noiseless tenor of their way.

Yet e'en these bones, from insult to protect,
    Some frail memorial still erected nigh,
With uncouth rhymes and shapeless sculpture deck'd,
    Implores the passing tribute of a sigh.

Their name, their years, spelt by the unletter'd Muse,
    The place of fame and elegy supply,
And many a holy text around she strews,
    That teach the rustic moralist to die.

For who, to dumb Forgetfulness a prey,
    This pleasing, anxious being e'er resign'd,
Left the warm precincts of the cheerful day,
    Nor cast one longing, lingering look behind?

On some fond breast the parting soul relies,
    Some pious drops the closing eye requires;
E'en from the tomb the voice of Nature cries,
    E'en in our ashes live their wonted fires.

For thee, who, mindful of the unhonour'd dead,
    Dost in those lines their artless tale relate,
If chance, by lonely Contemplation led,
    Some kindred spirit shall inquire thy fate,

Haply some hoary-headed swain may say,
    'Oft have we seen him, at the peep of dawn,
Brushing with hasty steps the dews away,
    To meet the sun upon the upland lawn.

There, at the foot of yonder nodding beech,
    That wreathes its old fantastic root so high,
His listless length at noontide would he stretch,
    And pore upon the brook that babbles by.

'Hard by yon wood, now smiling as in scorn,
    Muttering his wayward fancies, he would rove;
Now drooping, woeful, wan, like one forlorn,
    Or crazed with care, or cross'd in hopeless love.

'One morn I miss'd him on the accustom'd hill,
    Along the heath, and near his favourite tree;
Another came, nor yet beside the rill,
    Nor up the lawn, nor at the wood, was he:

'The next, with dirges due, in sad array,
    Slow through the churchway-path we saw him borne:
Approach, and read (for thou canst read) the lay
    Graved on the stone beneath yon aged thorn:'

The Epitaph.

Here rests his head upon the lap of Earth,
    A youth to Fortune and to Fame unknown:
Fair Science frown'd not on his humble birth,
    And Melancholy mark'd him for her own.

Large was his bounty, and his soul sincere;
    Heaven did a recompense as largely send:
He gave to misery all he had—a tear;
    He gain'd from Heaven—'twas all he wish'd—a friend.

No further seek his merits to disclose,
    Or draw his frailties from their dread abode,
(There they alike in trembling hope repose)
    The bosom of his Father and his God.

Excerpt from the Declaration of Independence of the Thirteen Colonies (1776)

This document, written largely by Thomas Jefferson, declared the United States
to be a free and sovereign country. It is filled with Enlightenment ideas about
the natural rights of man and the propriety of removing an oppressive government from power.

The unanimous Declaration of the thirteen United States of America.

When in the Course of human events, it becomes necessary for one people to dissolve the political bands which have connected them with another, and to assume among the powers of the earth, the separate and equal station to which the Laws of Nature and of Nature's God entitle them, a decent respect to the opinions of mankind requires that they should declare the causes which impel them to the separation.

Independence Hall
Philadelphia, Pennsylvania

We hold these truths to be self-evident:

- That all men are created equal, that they are endowed by their Creator with certain unalienable Rights, that among these are Life, Liberty and the pursuit of Happiness.
- That to secure these rights, Governments are instituted among Men, deriving their just powers from the consent of the governed,
- That whenever any Form of Government becomes destructive of these ends, it is the Right of the People to alter or to abolish it, and to institute new Government, laying its foundation on such principles and organizing its powers in such form, as to them shall seem most likely to effect their Safety and Happiness.

Prudence, indeed, will dictate that Governments long established should not be changed for light and transient causes; and accordingly all experience hath shewn, that mankind are more disposed to suffer, while evils are sufferable, than to right themselves by abolishing the forms to which they are accustomed. But when a long train of abuses and usurpations, pursuing invariably the same Object evinces a design to reduce them under absolute Despotism, it is their right, it is their duty, to throw off such Government, and to provide new Guards for their future security.

Such has been the patient sufferance of these Colonies; and such is now the necessity which constrains them to alter their former Systems of Government. The history of the present King of Great Britain is a history of repeated injuries and usurpations, all having in direct object the establishment of an absolute Tyranny over these States. To prove this, let Facts be submitted to a candid world. . . .

Glorious Things of Thee Are Spoken
by John Newton (1779)

John Newton, author of over 250 hymns, is best known as the writer of "Amazing Grace."

John Newton

Glorious things of thee are spoken,
Zion, city of our God!
He, Whose Word cannot be broken,
Formed thee for His own abode.
On the Rock of Ages founded,
What can shake thy sure repose?
With salvation's walls surrounded,
Thou may'st smile at all thy foes.

See! the streams of living waters,
Springing from eternal love;
Well supply thy sons and daughters,
And all fear of want remove:
Who can faint while such a river
Ever flows their thirst t'assuage?
Grace, which like the Lord, the Giver,
Never fails from age to age.

Round each habitation hovering,
See the cloud and fire appear!
For a glory and a cov'ring
Showing that the Lord is near.
Thus deriving from our banner
Light by night and shade by day;
Safe they feed upon the manna
Which He gives them when they pray.

Blest inhabitants of Zion,
Washed in the Redeemer's blood!
Jesus, Whom their souls rely on,
Makes them kings and priests to God.
'Tis His love His people raises,
Over self to reign as kings,
And as priests, His solemn praises
Each for a thank offering brings.

Savior, if of Zion's city,
I through grace a member am,
Let the world deride or pity,
I will glory in Thy Name.
Fading is the worldling's pleasure,
All his boasted pomp and show;
Solid joys and lasting treasure
None but Zion's children know.

To A Mouse, On Turning Her Up In Her Nest With The Plough by Robert Burns (1785)

Robert Burns (1759-1796) is the national poet of Scotland. In his short life he wrote a large body of work in the Scottish dialect that is filled with emotion, humor, and other traits that the Scots hold dear.

Wee, sleekit, cow'rin, tim'rous beastie,
O, what a panic's in thy breastie!
Thou need na start awa sae hasty,
Wi' bickering brattle!
I wad be laith to rin an' chase thee,
Wi' murd'ring pattle!

I'm truly sorry man's dominion,
Has broken nature's social union,
An' justifies that ill opinion,
Which makes thee startle
At me, thy poor, earth-born companion,
An' fellow-mortal!

I doubt na, whiles, but thou may thieve;
What then? poor beastie, thou maun live!
A daimen icker in a thrave
'S a sma' request;
I'll get a blessin wi' the lave,
An' never miss't!

Thy wee bit housie, too, in ruin!
It's silly wa's the win's are strewin!
An' naething, now, to big a new ane,
O' foggage green!
An' bleak December's winds ensuin,
Baith snell an' keen!

Thou saw the fields laid bare an' waste,
An' weary winter comin fast,
An' cozie here, beneath the blast,
Thou thought to dwell-
Till crash! the cruel coulter past
Out thro' thy cell.

That wee bit heap o' leaves an' stibble,
Has cost thee mony a weary nibble!
Now thou's turn'd out, for a' thy trouble,
But house or hald,
To thole the winter's sleety dribble,
An' cranreuch cauld!

But, Mousie, thou art no thy lane,
In proving foresight may be vain;
The best-laid schemes o' mice an' men
Gang aft agley,
An'lea'e us nought but grief an' pain,
For promis'd joy!

Still thou art blest, compar'd wi' me
The present only toucheth thee:
But, Och! I backward cast my e'e.
On prospects drear!
An' forward, tho' I canna see,
I guess an' fear!

The Lamb by William Blake

from *Songs of Innocence and Experience* (1789)

William Blake (1757-1827) was often misunderstood in his own day.
Some of his poems are hard to understand, but this one is simple enough.

Little Lamb, who made thee?
   Dost thou know who made thee?
Gave thee life, and bid thee feed
By the stream and o'er the mead;
Gave thee clothing of delight,
Softest clothing, wooly, bright;
Gave thee such a tender voice,
Making all the vales rejoice?
   Little Lamb, who made thee?
   Dost thou know who made thee?

   Little Lamb, I'll tell thee,
   Little Lamb, I'll tell thee:
He is called by thy name,
For He calls Himself a Lamb
He is meek, and He is mild,
He became a little child.
I a child, and thou a lamb,
We are called by His name.
   Little Lamb, God bless thee!
   Little Lamb, God bless thee!

The French Declaration of the Rights of Man and Citizen (1789)

*The National Assembly of France published the Declaration of the Rights of Man and Citizen,
which was written largely by the Marquis de Lafayette with help from Thomas Jefferson.
Louis XVI, king of France, refused to sign it.*

The representatives of the French people, organized as a National Assembly, considering that ignorance, neglect, or contempt of the rights of man are the only causes of public misfortunes and the corruption of governments, have resolved to set forth in a solemn declaration the natural, inalienable, and sacred rights of man in order that such declaration continually before all members of the social body may be a perpetual reminder of their rights and duties; in order that the acts of the legislative power and those of the executive power may constantly be compared with the aim of every political institution and may accordingly be more respected; in order that the demands of the citizens founded henceforth upon simple and incontestable principles may always be directed towards the maintenance of the Constitution and the welfare of all.

Accordingly, the National Assembly recognizes and proclaims in the presence and under the auspices of the Supreme Being the following rights of man and citizen.

1. Men are born and remain free and equal in rights; social distinctions may be based only upon general usefulness.

2. The aim of every political association is the preservation of the natural and inalienable rights of man; these rights are liberty, property, security and resistance to oppression.

3. The source of all sovereignty resides essentially in the nation; no group, no individual may exercise authority not emanating expressly therefrom.

4. Liberty consists of the power to do whatever is not injurious to others; thus the enjoyment of the natural rights of every man has for its limits only those that assure other members of society the enjoyment of those same rights; such limits may be determined only by law.

5. The law has the right to forbid only actions which are injurious to society. Whatever is not forbidden by law may not be prevented, and no one may be constrained to do what it does not prescribe.

6. Law is the expression of the general will; all citizens have the right to concur personally or through their representatives in its formation; it must be the same for all, whether it protects or punishes. All citizens being equal before it, are equally

admissible to all public offices, positions, and employments, according to their capacity, and without other distinction than that of virtues and talents.

7. No man may be accused, arrested, or detained except in the cases determined by law, and according to the forms prescribed thereby. Whoever solicits, expedites, or executes arbitrary orders or has them executed must be punished; but every citizen summoned or apprehended in pursuance of the law must obey immediately; he renders himself culpable by resistance.

8. The law is to establish only penalties that are absolutely and obviously necessary; and no one may be punished except by virtue of a law established and promulgated prior to the offense and legally applied.

9. Since every man is presumed innocent until declared guilty, if arrest be deemed indispensable, all unnecessary severity for securing the person of the accused must be severely repressed by law.

10. No one is to be disquieted because of his opinions, even religious, provided their manifestation does not disturb the public order established by law.

11. Free communication of ideas and opinions is one of the most precious of the rights of man. Consequently every citizen may speak, write, and print freely, subject to responsibility for the abuse of such liberty in the cases determined by law.

12. The guarantee of the rights of man and citizen necessitates a public force; such a force therefore, is instituted for the advantage of all and not for the particular benefit of those to whom it is entrusted.

13. For the maintenance of the public force and for the expenses of administration a common tax is indispensable; it must be assessed equally on all citizens in proportion to their means.

14. Citizens have the right to ascertain by themselves or through their representatives the necessity of the public tax, to consent to it freely, to supervise its use, and to determine its quota, assessment, payment, and duration.

15. Society has the right to require of every public agent an accounting of his administration.

16. Every society in which the guarantee of rights is not assured or the separation of powers not determined has no constitution at all.

17. Since property is a sacred and inviolable right, no one may be deprived thereof unless a legally established public necessity obviously requires it, and upon condition of a just and previous indemnity.

French Revolution of 1789

A Red, Red Rose by Robert Burns (1794)

O my Luve's like a red, red rose,
That's newly sprung in June:
O my Luve's like the melodie,
That's sweetly play'd in tune.

As fair art thou, my bonie lass,
So deep in luve am I;
And I will luve thee still, my dear,
Till a' the seas gang dry.

Till a' the seas gang dry, my dear,
And the rocks melt wi' the sun;
And I will luve thee still, my dear,
While the sands o' life shall run.

And fare-thee-weel, my only Luve!
And fare-thee-weel, a while!
And I will come again, my Luve,
Tho' 'twere ten thousand mile!

Auld Clay Biggin
Birthplace of Robert Burns
Alloway, Scotland

#7 from *Moods of My Own Mind*
by William Wordsworth (1807)

William Wordsworth (1770-1850), a leading figure in the Romantic movement, was one of the greatest English poets. He and other poets lived in the Lake District, a beautiful area in northwest England whose beauty influenced their love of nature. It is easy to see "a host of dancing Daffodils" in the Lake District.

I wandered lonely as a Cloud
That floats on high o'er Vales and Hills,
When all at once I saw a crowd
A host of dancing Daffodills;
Along the Lake, beneath the trees,
Ten thousand dancing in the breeze.

The waves beside them danced, but they
Outdid the sparkling waves in glee:–
A Poet could not but be gay
In such a laughing company:
I gaz'd—and gaz'd—but little thought
What wealth the show to me had brought:

For oft when on my couch I lie
In vacant or in pensive mood,
They flash upon that inward eye
Which is the bliss of solitude,
And then my heart with pleasure fills,
And dances with the Daffodils.

The Wolf and the Seven Little Kids from *Grimm's Household Tales* by the Brothers Grimm (1812, 1815)

Jakob and Wilhelm Grimm collected "Kinder-und Hausmärchen" (traditional German domestic tales) and published them in 1812 and 1815 (with subsequent revisions and additions). They collected most of the stories from German peasants, though some were Austrian and Swiss. Wilhelm was a librarian and a professor. Jakob was a linguist. The brothers lived in the same house and often studied the same subjects. In addition to Grimm's Household Tales, *they wrote a German dictionary. This version of "The Wolf and the Seven Little Kids" is from the Margaret Hunt translation of 1884.*

There was once upon a time an old goat who had seven little kids, and loved them with all the love of a mother for her children. One day she wanted to go into the forest and fetch some food. So she called all seven to her and said, "Dear children, I have to go into the forest, be on your guard against the wolf; if he come in, he will devour you all—skin, hair, and all. The wretch often disguises himself, but you will know him at once by his rough voice and his black feet." The kids said, "Dear mother, we will take good care of ourselves; you may go away without any anxiety." Then the old one bleated, and went on her way with an easy mind.

It was not long before some one knocked at the house-door and called, "Open the door, dear children; your mother is here, and has brought something back with her for each of you." But the little kids knew that it was the wolf, by the rough voice; "We will not open the door," cried they, "thou art not our mother. She has a soft, pleasant voice, but thy voice is rough; thou art the wolf!" Then the wolf went away to a shopkeeper and bought himself a great lump of chalk, ate this and made his voice soft with it. Then he came back, knocked at the door of the house, and cried, "Open the door, dear children, your mother is here and has brought something back with her for each of you." But the wolf had laid his black paws against the window, and the children saw them and cried, "We will not open the door, our mother has not black feet like thee; thou art the wolf." Then the wolf ran to a baker and said,

"I have hurt my feet, rub some dough over them for me." And when the baker had rubbed his feet over, he ran to the miller and said, "Strew some white meal over my feet for me." The miller thought to himself, "The wolf wants to deceive someone," and refused; but the wolf said, "If thou wilt not do it, I will devour thee." Then the miller was afraid, and made his paws white for him. Truly men are like that. So now the wretch went for the third time to

the house-door, knocked at it and said, "Open the door for me, children, your dear little mother has come home, and has brought every one of you something back from the forest with her." The little kids cried, "First show us thy paws that we may know if thou art our dear little mother." Then he put his paws in through the window, and when the kids saw that they were white, they believed that all he said was true, and opened the door. But who should come in but the wolf! They were terrified and wanted to hide themselves. One sprang under the table, the second into the bed, the third into the stove, the fourth into the kitchen, the fifth into the cupboard, the sixth under the washing-bowl, and the seventh into the clock-case. But the wolf found them all, and used no great ceremony; one after the other he swallowed them down his throat. The youngest, who was in the clock-case, was the only one he did not find. When the wolf had satisfied his appetite he took himself off, laid himself down under a tree in the green meadow outside, and began to sleep. Soon afterwards the old goat came home again from the forest. Ah! What a sight she saw there! The house-door stood wide open. The table, chairs, and benches were thrown down, the washing-bowl lay broken to pieces, and the quilts and pillows were pulled off the bed. She sought her children, but they were nowhere to be found. She called them one after another by name, but no one answered. At last, when she came to the youngest, a soft voice cried, "Dear mother, I am in the clock-case." She took the kid out, and it told her that the wolf had come and had eaten all the others. Then you may imagine how she wept over her poor children.

At length in her grief she went out, and the youngest kid ran with her. When they came to the meadow, there lay the wolf by the tree and snored so loud that the branches shook. She looked at him on every side and saw that something was moving and struggling in his gorged belly. "Ah, heavens," said she, "is it possible that my poor children whom he has swallowed down for his supper, can be still alive?" Then the kid had to run home and fetch scissors, and a needle and thread, and the goat cut open the monster's stomach, and hardly had she make one cut, than one little kid thrust its head out, and when she cut farther, all six sprang out one after another, and were all still alive, and had suffered no injury whatever, for in his greediness the monster had swallowed them down whole. What rejoicing there was! They embraced their dear mother, and jumped like a sailor at his wedding. The mother, however, said, "Now go and look for some big stones, and we will fill the wicked beast's stomach with them while he is still asleep." Then the seven kids dragged the stones thither with all speed, and put as many of them into his stomach as they could get in; and the mother sewed him up again in the greatest haste, so that he was not aware of anything and never once stirred. When the wolf at length had had his sleep out, he got on his legs, and as the stones in his stomach made him very thirsty, he wanted to go to a well to drink. But when he began to walk and move about, the stones in his stomach knocked against each other and rattled. Then cried he,

> "What rumbles and tumbles
> Against my poor bones?
> I thought 't was six kids,
> But it's naught but big stones."

And when he got to the well and stooped over the water and was just about to drink, the heavy stones made him fall in, and there was no help, but he had to drown miserably. When the seven kids saw that, they came running to the spot and cried aloud, "The wolf is dead! The wolf is dead!" and danced for joy round about the well with their mother.

Adoniram Judson's Rules of Holy Living (1819-1827)

Adoniram and Ann Judson were pioneering missionaries in Burma.
Adoniram developed an alphabet for the Burmese language and translated the Bible into Burmese.

Rules adopted on Sunday, April 4, 1819, the era of commencing public ministrations among the Burmans; revised and re-adopted on Saturday, December 9, 1820, and on Wednesday, April 25, 1821.

1. Be diligent in secret prayer, every morning and evening.
2. Never spend a moment in mere idleness.
3. Restrain natural appetites within the bounds of temperance and purity. "Keep thyself pure."
4. Suppress every emotion of anger and ill will.
5. Undertake nothing from motives of ambition, or love of fame.
6. Never do that which, at the moment, appears to be displeasing to God.
7. Seek opportunities of making some sacrifice for the good of others, especially of believers, provided the sacrifice is not inconsistent with some duty.
8. Endeavor to rejoice in every loss and suffering incurred for Christ's sake and the gospel's, remembering that though, like death, they are not to be wilfully incurred, yet, like death, they are great gain.

Re-adopted the above rules, particularly the 4th, on Sunday, August 31, 1823.

Re-adopted the above rules, particularly the 1st, on Sunday, October 29, 1826, and adopted the following minor rules:

1. Rise with the sun.
2. Read a certain portion of Burman every day, Sundays excepted.
3. Have the Scriptures and some devotional book in constant reading.
4. Read no book in English that has not a devotional tendency.
5. Suppress every unclean thought and look.

Revised and re-adopted all the above rules, particularly the second of the first class, on Sunday, March 11, 1827.

God grant me grace to keep the above rules, and ever live to His glory, for Jesus Christ's sake.

A. JUDSON.

The Elderbush by Hans Christian Andersen
(1805-1875)

Hans Christian Andersen was the son of a poor cobbler who died when Hans was eleven years old. After little schooling, he left his birthplace of Odense, Denmark and sought a career in theater in Copenhagen. In 1829, he began his writing career. During his career, he wrote humor, plays, poems, travel descriptions, and novels. A friend observed his great capacity for entertaining children and suggested he write down the stories he made up to entertain them. He published his first volume of fairy tales in 1835 and added to them year by year. During his lifetime, he was immensely popular in Denmark and in other countries.

Once upon a time there was a little boy who had taken cold. He had gone out and got his feet wet; though nobody could imagine how it had happened, for it was quite dry weather. So his mother undressed him, put him to bed, and had the tea-pot brought in, to make him a good cup of Elderflower tea. Just at that moment the merry old man came in who lived up a-top of the house all alone; for he had neither wife nor children—but he liked children very much, and knew so many fairy tales, that it was quite delightful.

"Now drink your tea," said the boy's mother; "then, perhaps, you may hear a fairy tale."

"If I had but something new to tell," said the old man. "But how did the child get his feet wet?"

"That is the very thing that nobody can make out," said his mother.

"Am I to hear a fairy tale?" asked the little boy.

"Yes, if you can tell me exactly—for I must know that first—how deep the gutter is in the little street opposite, that you pass through in going to school."

"Just up to the middle of my boot," said the child; "but then I must go into the deep hole."

"Ah, ah! That's where the wet feet came from," said the old man. "I ought now to tell you a story; but I don't know any more."

"You can make one in a moment," said the little boy. "My mother says that all you look at can be turned into a fairy tale and that you can find a story in everything."

"Yes, but such tales and stories are good for nothing. The right sort come of themselves; they tap at my forehead and say, 'Here we are.'"

"Won't there be a tap soon?" asked the little boy. And his mother laughed, put some Elder-flowers in the tea-pot, and poured boiling water upon them.

"Do tell me something! Pray do!"

"Yes, if a fairy tale would come of its own accord; but they are proud and haughty, and come only when they choose. Stop!" said he, all on a sudden. "I have it! Pay attention! There is one in the tea-pot!"

And the little boy looked at the tea-pot. The cover rose more and more; and the Elder-flowers came forth so fresh and white, and shot up long branches. Out of the spout even did they spread themselves on all sides, and grew larger and larger; it was a splendid Elderbush, a whole tree; and it reached into the very bed, and pushed the curtains aside. How it bloomed! And what an odour! In the middle of the bush sat a friendly-looking old woman in a most strange dress. It was quite green, like the leaves of the elder, and was trimmed with large white Elder-flowers; so that at first one could not tell whether it was a stuff, or a natural green and real flowers.

"What's that woman's name?" asked the little boy.

"The Greeks and Romans," said the old man, "called her a Dryad; but that we do not understand. The people who live in the New Booths [a row of buildings for seamen in Copenhagen] have a much better name for her; they call her 'old Granny'—and she it is to whom you are to pay attention. Now listen, and look at the beautiful Elderbush.

"Just such another large blooming Elder Tree stands near the New Booths. It grew there in the corner of a little miserable court-yard; and under it sat, of an afternoon, in the most splendid sunshine, two old people; an old, old seaman, and his old, old wife. They had great-grand-children, and were soon to celebrate the fiftieth anniversary of their marriage; but they could not exactly recollect the date: and old Granny sat in the tree, and looked as pleased as now. 'I know the date,' said she; but those below did not hear her, for they were talking about old times.

"'Yes, can't you remember when we were very little,' said the old seaman, 'and ran and played about? It was the very same court-yard where we now are, and we stuck slips in the ground, and made a garden.'

"'I remember it well,' said the old woman; 'I remember it quite well. We watered the slips, and one of them was an Elderbush. It took root, put forth green shoots, and grew up to be the large tree under which we old folks are now sitting.'

"'To be sure,' said he. 'And there in the corner stood a waterpail, where I used to swim my boats.'

"'True; but first we went to school to learn somewhat,' said she; 'and then we were confirmed. We both cried; but in the afternoon we went up the Round Tower, and looked down on Copenhagen, and far, far away over the water; then we went to Friedericksberg, where the King and the Queen were sailing about in their splendid barges.'

"'But I had a different sort of sailing to that, later; and that, too, for many a year; a long way off, on great voyages.'

"'Yes, many a time have I wept for your sake,' said she. 'I thought you were dead and gone, and lying down in the deep waters. Many a night have I got up to see if the wind had not changed: and changed it had, sure enough; but you never came. I remember so well one day, when the rain was pouring down in torrents, the scavengers were before the house where I was in service, and I had come up with the dust, and remained standing at the door—it was dreadful weather—when just as I was there, the postman came and gave me a letter. It was from you! What a tour that letter had made! I opened it instantly and read: I laughed and wept. I was so happy. In it I read that you were in warm lands where the coffee-tree grows. What a blessed land that must be! You related so much, and I saw it all the while the rain was pouring down, and I standing there with the dust-box. At the same moment came someone who embraced me.'

"'Yes; but you gave him a good box on his ear that made it tingle!'

"'But I did not know it was you. You arrived as soon as your letter, and you were so handsome—that you still are—and had a long yellow silk handkerchief round your neck, and a brand new hat on; oh, you were so dashing! Good heavens! What weather it was, and what a state the street was in!'

"'And then we married,' said he. 'Don't you remember? And then we had our first little boy, and then Mary, and Nicholas, and Peter, and Christian.'

"'Yes, and how they all grew up to be honest people, and were beloved by everybody.'

"'And their children also have children,' said the old sailor; 'yes, those are our grand-children, full of strength and vigor. It was, methinks about this season that we had our wedding.'

"'Yes, this very day is the fiftieth anniversary of the marriage,' said old Granny, sticking her head between the two old people; who thought it was their neighbor who nodded to them. They looked at each other and held one another by the hand. Soon after came their children, and their grand-children; for they knew well enough that it was the day of the fiftieth anniversary, and had come with their gratulations that very morning; but the old people had forgotten it, although they were able to remember all that had happened many years ago. And the Elderbush sent forth a strong odour in the sun, that was just about to set, and shone right in the old people's faces. They both looked so rosy-cheeked; and the youngest of the grandchildren danced around them, and called out quite delighted, that there was to be something very splendid that evening—they were all to have hot potatoes. And old Nanny nodded in the bush, and shouted 'hurrah!' with the rest."

"But that is no fairy tale," said the little boy, who was listening to the story.

"The thing is, you must understand it," said the narrator; "let us ask old Nanny."

"That was no fairy tale, 'tis true," said old Nanny; "but now it's coming. The most wonderful fairy tales grow out of that which is reality; were that not the case, you know, my magnificent Elderbush could not have grown out of the tea-pot." And then she took the little boy out of bed, laid him on her bosom, and the branches of the Elder Tree, full of flowers, closed around her. They sat in an aerial dwelling, and it flew with them through the air. Oh, it was wondrous beautiful! Old Nanny had grown all of a sudden a young and pretty maiden; but her robe was still the same green stuff with white flowers, which she had worn before. On her bosom she had a real Elderflower, and in her yellow waving hair a wreath of the flowers; her eyes were so large and blue that it was a pleasure to look at them; she kissed the boy, and now they were of the same age and felt alike.

Hand in hand they went out of the bower, and they were standing in the beautiful garden of their home. Near the green lawn papa's walking-stick was tied, and for the little ones it seemed to be endowed with life; for as soon as they got astride it, the round polished knob was turned into a magnificent neighing head, a long black mane fluttered in the breeze, and four slender yet strong legs shot out. The animal was strong and handsome, and away they went at full gallop round the lawn.

"Huzza! Now we are riding miles off," said the boy. "We are riding away to the castle where we were last year!"

And on they rode round the grass-plot; and the little maiden, who, we know, was no one else but old Nanny, kept on crying out, "Now we are in the country! Don't you see the farm-house yonder? And there is an Elder Tree standing beside it; and the cock is scraping away the earth for the hens, look, how he struts! And now we are close to the church. It lies high upon the hill, between the large oak-trees, one of which is half decayed. And now we are by the smithy, where the fire is blazing, and where the half-naked men are banging with their hammers till the sparks fly about. Away! away! To the beautiful country-seat!"

And all that the little maiden, who sat behind on the stick, spoke of, flew by in reality. The boy saw it all, and yet they were only going round the grass-plot. Then they played in a side avenue, and marked out a little garden on the earth; and they took Elder-blossoms from their hair, planted them, and they grew just like those the old people planted when they were children, as related before. They went hand in hand, as the old people had done when they were children; but not to the Round Tower, or to Friedericksberg; no, the little damsel wound her arms round the boy, and then they flew far away through all Denmark. And spring came, and summer; and then it was autumn, and then winter; and a thousand pictures were reflected in the eye and in the heart of the boy; and the little girl always sang to him, "This you will never forget." And during their whole flight the Elder Tree smelt so sweet and odorous; he remarked the roses and the fresh beeches, but the Elder Tree had a more wondrous fragrance, for its flowers hung on the breast of the little maiden; and there, too, did he often lay his head during the flight.

"It is lovely here in spring!" said the young maiden. And they stood in a beech-wood that had just put on its first green, where the woodroof at their feet sent forth its fragrance, and the pale-red anemony looked so pretty among the verdure. "Oh, would it were always spring in the sweetly-smelling Danish beech-forests!"

"It is lovely here in summer!" said she. And she flew past old castles of by-gone days of chivalry, where the red walls and the embattled gables were mirrored in the canal, where the swans were swimming, and peered up into the old cool avenues. In the fields the corn was waving like the sea; in the ditches red and yellow flowers were growing; while wild-drone flowers, and blooming convolvuluses were creeping in the hedges; and towards evening the moon rose round and large, and the haycocks in the meadows smelt so sweetly. "This one never forgets!"

"It is lovely here in autumn!" said the little maiden. And suddenly the atmosphere grew as blue again as before; the forest grew red, and green, and yellow-colored. The dogs came leaping along, and whole flocks of wild-fowl flew over the cairn, where blackberry-

bushes were hanging round the old stones. The sea was dark blue, covered with ships full of white sails; and in the barn old women, maidens, and children were sitting picking hops into a large cask; the young sang songs, but the old told fairy tales of mountain-sprites and soothsayers. Nothing could be more charming.

"It is delightful here in winter!" said the little maiden. And all the trees were covered with hoar-frost; they looked like white corals; the snow crackled under foot, as if one had new boots on; and one falling star after the other was seen in the sky. The Christmas-tree was lighted in the room; presents were there, and good-humor reigned. In the country the violin sounded in the room of the peasant; the newly-baked cakes were attacked; even the poorest child said, "It is really delightful here in winter!"

Yes, it was delightful; and the little maiden showed the boy everything; and the Elder Tree still was fragrant, and the red flag, with the white cross, was still waving: the flag under which the old seaman in the New Booths had sailed. And the boy grew up to be a lad, and was to go forth in the wide world-far, far away to warm lands, where the coffee-tree grows; but at his departure the little maiden took an Elder-blossom from her bosom, and gave it him to keep; and it was placed between the leaves of his Prayer-Book; and when in foreign lands he opened the book, it was always at the place where the keepsake-flower lay; and the more he looked at it, the fresher it became; he felt as it were, the fragrance of the Danish groves; and from among the leaves of the flowers he could distinctly see the little maiden, peeping forth with her bright blue eyes—and then she whispered, "It is delightful here in Spring, Summer, Autumn, and Winter"; and a hundred visions glided before his mind.

Thus passed many years, and he was now an old man, and sat with his old wife under the blooming tree. They held each other by the hand, as the old grand-father and grand-mother yonder in the New Booths did, and they talked exactly like them of old times, and of the fiftieth anniversary of their wedding. The little maiden, with the blue eyes, and with Elder-blossoms in her hair, sat in the tree, nodded to both of them, and said, "To-day is the fiftieth anniversary!" And then she took two flowers out of her hair, and kissed them. First, they shone like silver, then like gold; and when they laid them on the heads of the old people, each flower became a golden crown. So there they both sat, like a king and a queen, under the fragrant tree, that looked exactly like an elder: the old man told his wife the story of "Old Nanny," as it had been told him when a boy. And it seemed to both of them it contained much that resembled their own history; and those parts that were like it pleased them best.

"Thus it is," said the little maiden in the tree, "some call me 'Old Nanny,' others a 'Dryad,' but, in reality, my name is 'Remembrance'; 'tis I who sit in the tree that grows and grows! I can remember; I can tell things! Let me see if you have my flower still?"

And the old man opened his Prayer-Book. There lay the Elder-blossom, as fresh as if it had been placed there but a short time before; and Remembrance nodded, and the old people, decked with crowns of gold, sat in the flush of the evening sun. They closed their eyes, and—and—! Yes, that's the end of the story! The little boy lay in his bed; he did not know if he had dreamed or not, or if he had been listening while someone told him the story.

The tea-pot was standing on the table, but no Elder Tree was growing out of it! And the old man, who had been talking, was just on the point of going out at the door, and he did go.

"How splendid that was!" said the little boy. "Mother, I have been to warm countries."

"So I should think," said his mother. "When one has drunk two good cupfuls of Elder-flower tea, 'tis likely enough one goes into warm climates"; and she tucked him up nicely, least he should take cold. "You have had a good sleep while I have been sitting here, and arguing with him whether it was a story or a fairy tale."

"And where is old Nanny?" asked the little boy.

"In the tea-pot," said his mother; "and there she may remain."

Sonnet XLIII from *Sonnets from the Portuguese* by Elizabeth Barrett Browning (1847)

English poet Elizabeth Barrett (1806-1861) married another poet, Robert Browning, in 1846. They became perhaps the best-known husband and wife poets in English. They lived in Italy until her death.

How do I love thee? Let me count the ways.
I love thee to the depth and breadth and height
My soul can reach, when feeling out of sight
For the ends of Being and ideal Grace.
I love thee to the level of everyday's
Most quiet need, by sun and candlelight.
I love thee freely, as men strive for Right;
I love thee purely, as they turn from Praise.
I love thee with the passion put to use
In my old griefs, and with my childhood's faith.
I love thee with a love I seemed to lose
With my lost saints,—I love thee with the breath,
Smiles, tears, of all my life!—and, if God choose,
I shall but love thee better after death.

Rallying Speech
by Giuseppe Garibaldi (1860)

Giuseppe Garibaldi led Italian troops during the movement for the independence and unification of the Italian peninsula.

We must now consider the period which is just drawing to a close as almost the last stage of our national resurrection, and prepare ourselves to finish worthily the marvelous design of the elect of twenty generations, the completion of which Providence has reserved for this fortunate age.

Giuseppe Garibaldi

Yes, young men, Italy owes to you an undertaking which has merited the applause of the universe. You have conquered and you will conquer still, because you are prepared for the tactics that decide the fate of battles. You are not unworthy of the men who entered the ranks of a Macedonian phalanx, and who contended not in vain with the proud conquerors of Asia. To this wonderful page in our country's history another more glorious still will be added, and the slave shall show at last to his free brothers a sharpened sword forged from the links of his fetters.

To arms, then, all of you! all of you! And the oppressors and the mighty shall disappear like dust. You, too, women, cast away all the cowards from your embraces; they will give you only cowards for children, and you who are the daughters of the land of beauty must bear children who are noble and brave. Let timid doctrinaires depart from among us to carry their servility and their miserable fears elsewhere. This people is its own master. It wishes to be the brother of other peoples, but to look on the insolent with a proud glance, not to grovel before them imploring its own freedom. It will no longer follow in the trail of men whose hearts are foul. No! No! No!

Providence has presented Italy with Victor Emmanuel. Every Italian should rally round him. By the side of Victor Emmanuel every quarrel should be forgotten, all rancor depart. Once more I repeat my battle-cry: "To arms, all-all of you!" If March, 1861, does not find one million of Italians in arms, then alas for liberty, alas for the life of Italy. Ah, no, far be from me a thought which I loathe like poison. March of 1861, or if need be February, will find us all at our post-Italians of Calatafimi, Palermo, Ancona, the Volturno, Castelfidardo, and Isernia, and with us every man of this land who is not a coward or a slave. Let all of us rally round the glorious hero of Palestro and give the last blow to the crumbling edifice of tyranny. Receive, then, my gallant young volunteers, at the honored conclusion of ten battles, one word of farewell from me.

I utter this word with deepest affection and from the very bottom of my heart. Today I am obliged to retire, but for a few days only. The hour of battle will find me with you again, by the side of the champions of Italian liberty. Let those only return to their homes who are called by the imperative duties which they owe to their families, and those who by their glorious wounds have deserved the credit of their country. These, indeed, will serve Italy in their homes by their counsel, by the very aspect of the scars which adorn their youthful brows. Apart from these, let all others remain to guard our glorious banners. We shall meet again before long to march together to the redemption of our brothers who are still slaves of the stranger. We shall meet again before long to march to new triumphs.

Italian Peasant
Woman

The Charge of the Light Brigade
by Alfred, Lord Tennyson (1864)

Alfred, Lord Tennyson (1809-1892) was the most popular poet of the Victorian era.
He was Poet Laureate of England from 1850 until his death.
This poem memorialized a courageous but ill-advised charge against Russian troops
by the Light Brigade during the Crimean War against Russia.

Half a league, half a league,
Half a league onward,
All in the valley of Death
Rode the six hundred.
"Forward, the Light Brigade!
Charge for the guns!" he said:
Into the valley of Death
Rode the six hundred.

"Forward, the Light Brigade!"
Was there a man dismay'd?
Not tho' the soldier knew
Some one had blunder'd:
Their's not to make reply,
Their's not to reason why,
Their's but to do and die:
Into the valley of Death
Rode the six hundred.

Cannon to right of them,
Cannon to left of them,
Cannon in front of them
Volley'd and thunder'd;
Storm'd at with shot and shell,
Boldly they rode and well,
Into the jaws of Death,
Into the mouth of Hell
Rode the six hundred.

Flash'd all their sabres bare,
Flash'd as they turn'd in air
Sabring the gunners there,
Charging an army, while
All the world wonder'd:
Plunged in the battery-smoke
Right thro' the line they broke;
Cossack and Russian
Reel'd from the sabre-stroke
Shatter'd and sunder'd.
Then they rode back, but not,
Not the six hundred.

Cannon to right of them,
Cannon to left of them,
Cannon behind them
Volley'd and thunder'd;
Stormed at with shot and shell,
While horse and hero fell,
They that had fought so well
Came thro' the jaws of Death
Back from the mouth of Hell,
All that was left of them,
Left of six hundred.

When can their glory fade?
O the wild charge they made!
All the world wonder'd.
Honour the charge they made!
Honour the Light Brigade,
Noble six hundred!

Excerpt from *War and Peace*
by Leo Tolstoy (1865-1869)

*This epic novel by Russian author Leo Tolstoy explores life in Russia
around the time of Napoleon's invasion and includes Tolstoy's observations on history.
This excerpt describes a battle scene during the campaign.*

Leo Tolstoy

Book Ten: 1812, Chapter 39

Several tens of thousands of the slain lay in diverse postures and various uniforms on the fields and meadows belonging to the Davydov family and to the crown serfs – those fields and meadows where for hundreds of years the peasants of Borodino, Gorki, Shevardino, and Semenovsk had reaped their harvests and pastured their cattle. At the dressing stations the grass and earth were soaked with blood for a space of some three acres around. Crowds of men of various arms, wounded and unwounded, with frightened faces, dragged themselves back to Mozhaysk from the one army and back to Valuevo from the other. Other crowds, exhausted and hungry, went forward led by their officers. Others held their ground and continued to fire.

Over the whole field, previously so gaily beautiful with the glitter of bayonets and cloudlets of smoke in the morning sun, there now spread a mist of damp and smoke and a strange acid smell of saltpeter and blood. Clouds gathered and drops of rain began to fall on the dead and wounded, on the frightened, exhausted, and hesitating men, as if to say: "Enough, men! Enough! Cease . . . bethink yourselves! What are you doing?"

To the men of both sides alike, worn out by want of food and rest, it began equally to appear doubtful whether they should continue to slaughter one another; all the faces expressed hesitation, and the question arose in every soul: "For what, for whom, must I kill and be killed? . . . You may go and kill whom you please, but I don't want to do so anymore!" By evening this thought had ripened in every soul. At any moment these men might have been seized with horror at what they were doing and might have thrown up everything and run away anywhere.

But though toward the end of the battle the men felt all the horror of what they were doing, though they would have been glad to leave off, some incomprehensible, mysterious power continued to control them, and they still brought up the charges, loaded, aimed, and applied the match, though only one artilleryman survived out of every three, and though they stumbled and panted with fatigue, perspiring and stained with blood and powder. The cannon balls flew just as swiftly and cruelly from both sides, crushing human bodies, and that terrible work which was not done by the will of a man but at the will of Him who governs men and worlds continued.

Anyone looking at the disorganized rear of the Russian army would have said that, if only the French made one more slight effort, it would disappear; and anyone looking at the rear of the French army would have said that the Russians need only make one more slight effort and the French would be destroyed. But neither the French nor the Russians made that effort, and the flame of battle burned slowly out.

The Russians did not make that effort because they were not attacking the French. At the beginning of the battle they stood blocking the way to Moscow and they still did so at the end of the battle as at the beginning. But even had the aim of the Russians been to drive the French from their positions, they could not have made this last effort, for all the Russian troops had been broken up, there was no part of the Russian army that had not suffered in the battle, and though still holding their positions they had lost ONE HALF of their army.

The French, with the memory of all their former victories during fifteen years, with the assurance of Napoleon's invincibility, with the consciousness that they had captured part of the battlefield and had lost only a quarter of their men and still had their Guards intact, twenty thousand strong, might easily have made that effort. The French had attacked the Russian army in order to drive it from its position and ought to have made that effort, for as long as the Russians continued to block the road to Moscow as before, the aim of the French had not been attained and all their efforts and losses were in vain. But the French did not make that effort. Some historians say that

Napoleon and Soldiers

Napoleon need only have used his Old Guards, who were intact, and the battle would have been won. To speak of what would have happened had Napoleon sent his Guards is like talking of what would happen if autumn became spring. It could not be. Napoleon did not give his Guards, not because he did not want to, but because it could not be done. All the generals, officers, and soldiers of the French army knew it could not be done, because the flagging spirit of the troops would not permit it.

It was not Napoleon alone who had experienced that nightmare feeling of the mighty arm being stricken powerless, but all the generals and soldiers of his army whether they had taken part in the battle or not, after all their experience of previous battles—when after one

Moscow

tenth of such efforts the enemy had fled—experienced a similar feeling of terror before an enemy who, after losing HALF his men, stood as threateningly at the end as at the beginning of the battle. The moral force of the attacking French army was exhausted. Not that sort of victory which is defined by the capture of pieces of material fastened to sticks, called standards, and of the ground on which the troops had stood and were standing, but a moral victory that convinces the enemy of the moral superiority of his opponent and of his own impotence was gained by the Russians at Borodino. The French invaders, like an infuriated animal that has in its onslaught received a mortal wound, felt that they were perishing, but could not stop, any more than the Russian army, weaker by one half, could help swerving. By impetus gained, the French army was still able to roll forward to Moscow, but there, without further effort on the part of the Russians, it had to perish, bleeding from the mortal wound it had received at Borodino. The direct consequence of the battle of Borodino was Napoleon's senseless flight from Moscow, his retreat along the old Smolensk road, the destruction of the invading army of five hundred thousand men, and the downfall of Napoleonic France, on which at Borodino for the first time the hand of an opponent of stronger spirit had been laid.

Excerpt from *The Nile Tributaries of Abyssinia* by Samuel W. Baker (1867)

Samuel Baker explored the rivers and streams that feed the Nile River. He made an expedition to Abyssinia (modern Ethiopia) in 1861-62 with his wife and a team of companions.

Our camp was in a favourable locality, well shaded by large trees, on the margin of a small stream; this was nearly dry at this season, and the water was extremely bad, having a strong taste of copper. I had remarked throughout the neighbourhood unmistakeable evidences of the presence of this metal—the surface of the rocks was in many places bright green, like malachite, and, upon an exploration of the bed of the stream, I

Abyssinia

found veins of a green substance in the perpendicular cliffs that had been cut through by the torrent. These green veins passed through a bed of reddish, hard rock, glistening with minute crystals, which I believe to have been copper. There is no doubt that much might be done were the mineral wealth of this country thoroughly investigated.

The day following our arrival was passed in receiving visits from a number of Abyssinians, and the head men of Mek Nimmur. There was a mixture of people, as many of the Jaleen Arabs who had committed some crime in the Egyptian territory, had fled across the country and joined the exiled chief of their tribe. Altogether, the society in this district was not *creme de la creme*, as Mek Nimmur's territory was an asylum for all the blackguards of the adjoining countries, who were attracted by the excitement and lawlessness of continual border warfare. The troop that we had seen at Ombrega returned with a hundred and two head of camels, that they had stolen from the west bank of the Atbara. Mounted upon hygeens, Mek Nimmur's irregulars thought nothing of marching sixty miles in one day; thus their attack and retreat were equally sudden and unexpected.

I had a quantity of rhinoceros hide in pieces of the size required for shields; these were much prized in this fighting country, and I presented them to a number of head men who had honoured us with a visit. I begged them to guide two of my people to the presence of Mek Nimmur, with a preliminary message. This they promised to perform. Accordingly, I sent Taher Noor and Bacheet on horseback, with a most polite message, accompanied with my card in an envelope, and a small parcel, carefully wrapped in four or five different papers;

this contained a very beautiful Persian lance-head, of polished steel inlaid with gold, that I had formerly purchased at Constantinople.

During their absence, we were inundated with visitors, the Abyssinians, in their tight pantaloons, contrasting strongly with the loosely-clad Arabs. In about an hour, my messengers returned, accompanied by two men on horseback, with a hospitable message from Mek Nimmur, and an invitation to pay him a visit at his own residence. I had some trifling present ready for everybody of note, and, as Taher Noor and my people had already explained all they knew concerning us, Mek Nimmur's suspicions had entirely vanished.

As we were conversing with Mek Nimmur's messengers through the medium of Taher Noor, who knew their language, our attention was attracted by the arrival of a tremendous swell who at a distance I thought must be Mek Nimmur himself. A snow-white mule carried an equally snow-white person, whose tight white pantaloons looked as though he had forgotten his trousers, and had mounted in his drawers. He carried a large umbrella to shade his complexion; a pair of handsome silver-mounted pistols were arranged upon his saddle, and a silver-hilted curved sword, of the peculiar Abyssinian form, hung by his side. This grand personage was followed by an attendant, also mounted upon a mule, while several men on foot accompanied them, one of whom carried his lance and shield. Upon a near approach, he immediately dismounted, and advanced towards us, bowing in a most foppish manner, while his attendant followed him on foot with an enormous violin, which he immediately handed to him. This fiddle was very peculiar in shape, being a square, with an exceedingly long neck extending from one corner; upon this was stretched a solitary string, and the bow was very short and much bent. This was an Abyssinian Paganini. He was a professional minstrel of the highest grade, who had been sent by Mek Nimmur to welcome us on our arrival.

These musicians are very similar to the minstrels of ancient times; they attend at public rejoicings, and at births, deaths, and marriages of great personages, upon which occasions they extemporize their songs according to circumstances. My hunting in the Base country formed his theme, and for at least an hour he sang of my deeds, in an extremely loud and disagreeable voice, while he accompanied himself upon his fiddle, which he held downwards like a violoncello: during the whole of his song he continued in movement, marching with a sliding step to the front, and gliding to the right and left in a manner that, if intended to be graceful, was extremely comic. The substance of this minstrelsy was explained to me by Taher Noor, who listened eagerly to the words, which he translated with evident satisfaction. Of course, like all minstrels, he was an absurd flatterer, and, having gathered a few facts for his theme, he wandered slightly from the truth in his poetical description of my deeds.

He sang of me as though I had been Richard Coeur de Lion, and recounted, before an admiring throng of listeners, how "I had wandered with a young wife from my own distant country to fight the terrible Base; how I had slain them in single combat; and how elephants and lions were struck down like lambs and kids by my hands; that during my absence in the hunt, my wife had been carried off by the Base; that I had, on my return to my pillaged camp, galloped off in chase, and, overtaking the enemy, hundreds had fallen by my rifle and sword, and I had liberated and recovered the lady, who now had arrived safe with her lord in the country of the great Mek Nimmur," &c. &c. &c.

This was all very pretty, no doubt, and as true as most poetical and musical descriptions, but I felt certain that there must be something to pay for this flattering entertainment; if you are considered to be a great man, a present is invariably expected in proportion to your importance. I suggested to Taher Noor that I must give him a couple of dollars. "What!" said Taher Noor, "A couple of dollars! Impossible! A musician of his standing is accustomed to receive thirty and forty dollars from great people for so beautiful and honourable a song."

This was somewhat startling; I began to reflect upon the price of a box at Her Majesty's Theatre in London; but there I was not the hero of the opera; this minstrel combined the whole affair in a most simple manner; he was Verdi, Costa, and orchestra all in one; he was a thorough Macaulay as historian, therefore I had to pay the composer as well as the fiddler. I compromised the matter, and gave him a few dollars, as I understood that he was Mek Nimmur's private minstrel, but I never parted with my dear Maria Theresa [the Austrian dollar, that is the only large current coin in that country] with so much regret as upon that occasion, and I begged him not to incommode himself by paying us another visit, or, should he be obliged to do so, I trusted he would not think it necessary to bring his violin.

The minstrel retired in the same order that he had arrived, and I watched his retreating figure with unpleasant reflections, that were suggested by doubts as to whether I had paid him too little or too much; Taher Noor thought that he was underpaid; my own opinion was, that I had brought a curse upon myself equal to a succession of London organ-grinders, as I fully expected that other minstrels, upon hearing of the Austrian dollars, would pay us a visit, and sing of my great deeds.

In the afternoon, we were sitting beneath the shade of our tamarind tree when we thought we could perceive our musical friend returning. As he drew near, we were convinced that it was the identical minstrel, who had most probably been sent with a message from Mek Nimmur: there he was, in snow-white raiment, on the snow-white mule, with the mounted attendant and the violin as before. He dismounted upon arrival opposite the camp, and approached with his usual foppish bow; but we looked on

Ethiopian Village

in astonishment: it was not our Paganini, it was ANOTHER MINSTREL! who was determined to sing an ode in our praise. I felt that this was an indirect appeal to Maria Theresa, and I at once declared against music. I begged him not to sing; "my wife had a headache—I disliked the fiddle—could he play anything else instead?" and I expressed a variety of polite excuses, but to no purpose; he insisted upon singing; if I "disliked the fiddle, he would sing without an accompaniment, but he could not think of insulting so great a man as myself by returning without an ode to commemorate our arrival."

I was determined that he should NOT sing; he was determined that he WOULD, therefore I desired him to leave my camp; this he agreed to do, provided I would allow him to cross the stream, and sing to my Tokrooris, in my praise, beneath a neighbouring tree about fifty yards distant. He remounted his mule with his violin, to ford the muddy stream, and he descended the steep bank, followed by his attendant on foot, who drove the unwilling mule.

Upon arrival at the brink of the dirty brook, that was about three feet deep, the mule positively refused to enter the water, and stood firm with its fore feet sunk deep in the mud. The attendant attempted to push it on behind, at the same time he gave it a sharp blow with his sheathed sword; this changed the scene to the "opera comique." In one instant the mule gave so vigorous and unexpected a kick into the bowels of the attendant, that he fell upon his back, heels uppermost, while at the same moment the minstrel, in his snow-white garments, was precipitated head foremost into the muddy brook, and for the moment disappearing, the violin alone could be seen floating on the surface. A second later, a wretched-looking object, covered with slime and filth, emerged from the slough; this was Paganini the second! who, after securing his fiddle, that had stranded on a mud-bank, scrambled up the steep slope, amidst the roars of laughter of my people and of ourselves; while the perverse mule, having turned harmony into discord, kicked up its heels and galloped off, braying an ode in praise of liberty, as the "Lay of the last Minstrel." The discomfited fiddler was wiped down by my Tokrooris, who occasionally burst into renewed fits of laughter during the operation; the mule was caught, and the minstrel remounted, and returned home completely out of tune.

Real Faith

by George Müller (c. 1872)

TEXT: "Faith is the substance of things hoped for, the evidence of things not seen. Through faith we understand that the worlds were framed by the Word of God, so that things which are seen were not made of things which do appear" (Hebrews 11:1).

FIRST: WHAT IS FAITH? In the simplest manner in which I am able to express it, I answer: Faith is the assurance that the thing which God has said in His Word is true, and that God will act according to what He has said in His Word. This assurance, this reliance on God's Word, this confidence is FAITH.

NO IMPRESSIONS ARE TO BE TAKEN IN CONNECTION WITH FAITH. Impressions have neither one thing nor the other to do with faith. Faith has to do with the Word of God. It is not impressions, strong or weak, which will make any difference. We have to do with the written Word and not ourselves or our impressions.

George Müller

PROBABILITIES ARE NOT TO BE TAKEN INTO ACCOUNT. Many people are willing to believe regarding those things that seem probable to them. Faith has nothing to do with probabilities. The province of FAITH begins where probabilities cease and sight and sense fail. A great many of God's children are cast down and lament their want of Faith. They write to me and say that they have no impressions, no feeling, they see no probability that the thing they wish will come to pass. APPEARANCES ARE NOT TO BE TAKEN INTO ACCOUNT. The question is—whether God has spoken it in His Word.

And now, beloved Christian friends, you are in great need to ask yourselves whether you are in the habit of thus confiding, in your inmost soul, in what God has said, and whether you are in earnest in seeking to find whether the thing you want is in accordance with what He has said in His Word.

SECOND: HOW FAITH MAY BE INCREASED. God delights to increase the Faith of His children. Our Faith which is feeble at first, is developed and strengthened more and more by us. We ought, instead of wanting no trials before victory, no exercise for patience, to be willing to take them from God's hand as a means. I say—and say it deliberately—trials, obstacles, difficulties, and sometimes defeats, are the very food of Faith. I get letters from so many of God's dear children who say: "Dear Brother Müller, I'm writing this because I am so weak in faith." Just so surely as we ask to have our Faith strengthened, we must feel a willingness to take from God's hand the means for strengthening it. We must allow Him to educate us through trials and bereavements and troubles. It is through trials that Faith is exercised and developed more and more. God affectionately permits difficulties, that He may develop unceasingly that which He is willing to do for us, and to this end we should not shrink, but if He gives us sorrow and hindrances and losses and afflictions, we should take them out of His hands as evidences of His love and care for us in developing more and more that Faith which He is seeking to strengthen in us.

The Church of God is not aroused to see God as the beautiful and lovable One He is, and hence the littleness of blessedness. Oh, beloved brothers and sisters in Christ, seek to learn for yourselves, for I cannot tell you the blessedness! In the darkest moments I am able to confide in Him, for I know what a beautiful and kind and lovable Being He is, and, if it be the will of God to put us in the furnace, let Him do it, that so we may acquaint ourselves with Him as He will reveal Himself, and that we may know Him better. We come then to the conclusion that God is a lovable Being, and we are satisfied with Him, and say: "It is my Father, let Him do as He pleases."

When I first began to allow God to deal with me, relying on Him, taking Him at His Word, and set out fifty years ago simply relying on Him for myself, family, taxes, travelling expenses and every other need, I rested on the simple promises I found in the sixth chapter of Matthew. Read Matthew 6:25-34 carefully. I believed the Word, I rested on it and practiced it. I took God at His word. A stranger, a foreigner in England, I knew seven languages and might have used them perhaps as a means of remunerative employment but I had consecrated myself to labor for the Lord, I put my reliance in the God who has promised, and He has acted according to His Word. I've lacked nothing—nothing. I have had my trials, my difficulties, and my purse empty, but my receipts have aggregated thousands of dollars, while the work has gone on these 51 years. Then, with regard to my pastoral work, for the past 51 years I have had great difficulties, great trials and perplexities. There will always be difficulties, always trials. But God has sustained me under them and delivered now out of them, and the work has gone on. Now, this is not, as some have said, because I am a man of great mental power, or endowed with energy and perseverance—these are not the reasons. It is because I have confided in God; because I have sought God, and He has cared for the Institution, which, under His direction, has 100 schools, with masters and mistresses and other departments which I have told you before.

I do not carry the burden. And now in my 67th year, I have physical strength and mental vigor for as much work as when I was a young man in the university, studying and preparing Latin orations. I am just as vigorous as at that time. How comes this? Because in

the last half century of labor I've been able, with the simplicity of a child, to rely upon God. I have had my trials, but I have laid hold upon God, and so it has come to pass that I have been sustained. It is not only permission, but positive command that He gives, to cast the burdens upon Him. Oh, let us do it! My beloved brothers and sisters in Christ, "Cast thy burden upon the Lord and He shall sustain thee." Day by day I do it. This morning sixty matters in connection with the church of which I am pastor, I brought before the Lord, and thus it is, day by day I do it, and year by year; ten years, thirty years, forty years.

Do not, however, expect to obtain full Faith at once. All such things as jumping into full exercise of Faith in such things I discountenance. I do not believe in it. I do not believe in it. I DO NOT BELIEVE IN IT, AND I WISH YOU PLAINLY TO UNDERSTAND I DO NOT BELIEVE IN IT. All such things go on in a natural way. The little I did obtain, I did not obtain all at once. All this I say particularly, because letters come to me full of questions from those who seek to have their Faith strengthened. Begin over again, staying your soul on the Word of God, and you will have an increase of your Faith as you exercise it.

One thing more. Some say, "Oh, I shall never have the gift of Faith Mr. Müller has got." This is a mistake—it is the greatest error—there is not a particle of truth in it. My Faith is the same kind of Faith that all of God's children have had. It is the same kind that Simon Peter had, and all Christians may obtain the like Faith. My Faith is their Faith, though there may be more of it because my Faith has been a little more developed by exercise then theirs; but their Faith is precisely the Faith I exercise, only, with regard to degree, mine may be more strongly exercised.

Now, my beloved brothers and sisters, begin in a little way.

At first I was able to trust the Lord for ten dollars, then for a hundred dollars, then for a thousand dollars, and now, with the greatest ease, I could trust Him for a million dollars, if there was occasion. But first, I should quietly, carefully, deliberately examine and see whether what I was trusting for, was something in accordance with His promises in His written Word.

"As laborers together with Him" (2 Corinthians 6:1).

The Necklace

by Guy de Maupassant (1884)

She was one of those pretty and charming girls who are sometimes, as if by a mistake of destiny, born in a family of clerks. She had no dowry, no expectations, no means of being known, understood, loved, wedded, by any rich and distinguished man; and she let herself be married to a little clerk at the Ministry of Public Instruction.

She dressed plainly because she could not dress well, but she was as unhappy as though she had really fallen from her proper station; since with women there is neither caste nor rank; and beauty, grace, and charm act instead of family and birth. Natural fineness, instinct for what is elegant, suppleness of wit, are the sole hierarchy, and make from women of the people the equals of the very greatest ladies.

She suffered ceaselessly, feeling herself born for all the delicacies and all the luxuries. She suffered from the poverty of her dwelling, from the wretched look of the walls, from the worn-out chairs, from the ugliness of the curtains. All those things, of which another woman of her rank would never even have been conscious, tortured her and made her angry. The sight of the little Breton peasant who did her humble housework aroused in her regrets which were despairing, and distracted dreams. She thought of the silent ante-chambers hung with Oriental tapestry, lit by tall bronze candelabra, and of the two great footmen in knee-breeches who sleep in the big armchairs, made drowsy by the heavy warmth of the hot-air stove. She thought of the long salons fitted up with ancient silk, of the delicate furniture carrying priceless curiosities, and of the coquettish perfumed boudoirs made for talks at five o'clock with intimate friends, with men famous and sought after, whom all women envy and whose attention they all desire.

When she sat down to dinner, before the round table covered with a table-cloth three days old, opposite her husband, who uncovered the soup tureen and declared with an enchanted air, "Ah, the good pot-au-feu! I don't know anything better than that," she thought of dainty dinners, of shining silverware, of tapestry which peopled the walls with ancient personages and with strange birds flying in the midst  of a fairy forest; and she thought of delicious dishes served on marvelous plates, and of the whispered gallantries which you listen to with a sphinx-like smile, while you are eating the pink flesh of a trout or the wings of a quail.

She had no dresses, no jewels, nothing. And she loved nothing but that; she felt made for that. She would so have liked to please, to be envied, to be charming, to be sought after.

She had a friend, a former schoolmate at the convent, who was rich, and whom she did not like to go and see any more, because she suffered so much when she came back.

But, one evening, her husband returned home with a triumphant air, and holding a large envelope in his hand.

"There," said he, "here is something for you."

She tore the paper sharply, and drew out a printed card which bore these words:

"The Minister of Public Instruction and Mme. Georges Ramponneau request the honor of M. and Mme. Loisel's company at the palace of the Ministry on Monday evening, January 18th."

Instead of being delighted, as her husband hoped, she threw the invitation on the table with disdain, murmuring:

"What do you want me to do with that?"

"But, my dear, I thought you would be glad. You never go out, and this is such a fine opportunity. I had awful trouble to get it. Every one wants to go; it is very select, and they are not giving many invitations to clerks. The whole official world will be there."

She looked at him with an irritated eye, and she said, impatiently:

"And what do you want me to put on my back?"

He had not thought of that; he stammered:

"Why the dress you go to the theater in. It looks very well, to me."

He stopped, distracted, seeing that his wife was crying. Two great tears descended slowly from the corners of her eyes towards the corners of her mouth. He stuttered:

"What's the matter? What's the matter?"

But, by a violent effort, she had conquered her grief, and she replied, with a calm voice, while she wiped her wet cheeks:

"Nothing. Only I have no dress, and therefore I can't go to this ball. Give your card to some colleague whose wife is better equipped than I."

He was in despair. He resumed:

"Come, let us see, Mathilde. How much would it cost, a suitable dress, which you could use on other occasions, something very simple?"

She reflected several seconds, making her calculations and wondering also what sum she could ask without drawing on herself an immediate refusal and a frightened exclamation from the economical clerk.

Finally, she replied, hesitatingly:

"I don't know exactly, but I think I could manage it with four hundred francs."

He had grown a little pale, because he was laying aside just that amount to buy a gun and treat himself to a little shooting next summer on the plain of Nanterre, with several friends who went to shoot larks down there, of a Sunday.

But he said:

"All right. I will give you four hundred francs. And try to have a pretty dress."

The day of the ball drew near, and Mme. Loisel seemed sad, uneasy, anxious. Her dress was ready, however. Her husband said to her one evening:

"What is the matter? Come, you've been so queer these last three days."

And she answered:

"It annoys me not to have a single jewel, not a single stone, nothing to put on. I shall look like distress. I should almost rather not go at all."

He resumed:

"You might wear natural flowers. It's very stylish at this time of the year. For ten francs you can get two or three magnificent roses."

She was not convinced.

"No; there's nothing more humiliating than to look poor among other women who are rich."

But her husband cried:

"How stupid you are! Go look up your friend Mme. Forestier, and ask her to lend you some jewels. You're quite thick enough with her to do that."

She uttered a cry of joy:

"It's true. I never thought of it."

The next day she went to her friend and told of her distress.

Mme. Forestier went to a wardrobe with a glass door, took out a large jewel-box, brought it back, opened it, and said to Mme. Loisel:

"Choose, my dear."

She saw first of all some bracelets, then a pearl necklace, then a Venetian cross, gold, and precious stones of admirable workmanship. She tried on the ornaments before the glass, hesitated, could not make up her mind to part with them, to give them back. She kept asking:

"Haven't you any more?"

"Why, yes. Look. I don't know what you like."

All of a sudden she discovered, in a black satin box, a superb necklace of diamonds; and her heart began to beat with an immoderate desire. Her hands trembled as she took it. She fastened it around her throat, outside her high-necked dress, and remained lost in ecstasy at the sight of herself.

Then she asked, hesitating, filled with anguish:

"Can you lend me that, only that?"

"Why, yes, certainly."

She sprang upon the neck of her friend, kissed her passionately, then fled with her treasure.

The day of the ball arrived. Mme. Loisel made a great success. She was prettier than them all, elegant, gracious, smiling, and crazy with joy. All the men looked at her, asked her name, endeavored to be introduced. All the attachés of the Cabinet wanted to waltz with her. She was remarked by the minister himself.

She danced with intoxication, with passion, made drunk by pleasure, forgetting all, in the triumph of her beauty, in the glory of her success, in a sort of cloud of happiness composed of all this homage, of all this admiration, of all these awakened desires, and of that sense of complete victory which is so sweet to woman's heart.

She went away about four o'clock in the morning. Her husband had been sleeping since midnight, in a little deserted ante-room, with three other gentlemen whose wives were having a very good time.

He threw over her shoulders the wraps which he had brought, modest wraps of common life, whose poverty contrasted with the elegance of the ball dress. She felt this and wanted to escape so as not to be remarked by the other women, who were enveloping themselves in costly furs.

Loisel held her back.

"Wait a bit. You will catch cold outside. I will go and call a cab."

But she did not listen to him, and rapidly descended the stairs. When they were in the street they did not find a carriage; and they began to look for one, shouting after the cabmen whom they saw passing by at a distance.

They went down towards the Seine, in despair, shivering with cold. At last they found on the quay one of those ancient noctambulant coupés which, exactly as if they were ashamed to show their misery during the day, are never seen round Paris until after nightfall.

It took them to their door in the Rue des Martyrs, and once more, sadly, they climbed up homeward. All was ended for her. And as to him, he reflected that he must be at the Ministry at ten o'clock.

She removed the wraps, which covered her shoulders, before the glass, so as once more to see herself in all her glory. But suddenly she uttered a cry. She had no longer the necklace around her neck!

Her husband, already half-undressed, demanded:

"What is the matter with you?"

She turned madly towards him:

"I have—I have—I've lost Mme. Forestier's necklace."

He stood up, distracted.

"What!—how?—Impossible!"

And they looked in the folds of her dress, in the folds of her cloak, in her pockets, everywhere. They did not find it.

He asked:

"You're sure you had it on when you left the ball?"

"Yes, I felt it in the vestibule of the palace."

"But if you had lost it in the street we should have heard it fall. It must be in the cab."

"Yes. Probably. Did you take his number?"

"No. And you, didn't you notice it?"

"No."

They looked, thunderstruck, at one another. At last Loisel put on his clothes.

"I shall go back on foot," said he, "over the whole route which we have taken, to see if I can't find it."

And he went out. She sat waiting on a chair in her ball dress, without strength to go to bed, overwhelmed, without fire, without a thought.

Her husband came back about seven o'clock. He had found nothing.

He went to Police Headquarters, to the newspaper offices, to offer a reward; he went to the cab companies—everywhere, in fact, whither he was urged by the least suspicion of hope.

She waited all day, in the same condition of mad fear before this terrible calamity.

Loisel returned at night with a hollow, pale face; he had discovered nothing.

"You must write to your friend," said he, "that you have broken the clasp of her necklace and that you are having it mended. That will give us time to turn round."

She wrote at his dictation.

At the end of a week they had lost all hope.

And Loisel, who had aged five years, declared:

"We must consider how to replace that ornament."

The next day they took the box which had contained it, and they went to the jeweler whose name was found within. He consulted his books.

"It was not I, madame, who sold that necklace; I must simply have furnished the case."

Then they went from jeweler to jeweler, searching for a necklace like the other, consulting their memories, sick both of them with chagrin and with anguish.

They found, in a shop at the Palais Royal, a string of diamonds which seemed to them exactly like the one they looked for. It was worth forty thousand francs. They could have it for thirty-six.

So they begged the jeweler not to sell it for three days yet. And they made a bargain that he should buy it back for thirty-four thousand francs, in case they found the other one before the end of February.

Loisel possessed eighteen thousand francs which his father had left him. He would borrow the rest.

He did borrow, asking a thousand francs of one, five hundred of another, five louis here, three louis there. He gave notes, took up ruinous obligations, dealt with usurers, and all the race of lenders. He compromised all the rest of his life, risked his signature without even knowing if he could meet it; and, frightened by the pains yet to come, by the black misery which was about to fall upon him, by the prospect of all the physical privations and of all the moral tortures which he was to suffer, he went to get the new necklace, putting down upon the merchant's counter thirty-six thousand francs.

When Mme. Loisel took back the necklace Mme. Forestier said to her, with a chilly manner:

"You should have returned it sooner, I might have needed it."

She did not open the case, as her friend had so much feared. If she had detected the substitution, what would she have thought, what would she have said? Would she not have taken Mme. Loisel for a thief?

Mme. Loisel now knew the horrible existence of the needy. She took her part, moreover, all on a sudden, with heroism. That dreadful debt must be paid. She would pay it. They dismissed their servant; they changed their lodgings; they rented a garret under the roof.

She came to know what heavy housework meant and the odious cares of the kitchen. She washed the dishes, using her rosy nails on the greasy pots and pans. She washed the dirty linen, the shirts, and the dish-cloths, which she dried upon a line; she carried the slops down to the street every morning, and carried up the water, stopping for breath at every landing. And, dressed like a woman of the people, she went to the fruiterer, the grocer, the butcher, her basket on her arm, bargaining, insulted, defending her miserable money sou by sou.

Each month they had to meet some notes, renew others, obtain more time.

Her husband worked in the evening making a fair copy of some tradesman's accounts, and late at night he often copied manuscript for five sous a page.

And this life lasted ten years.

At the end of ten years they had paid everything, everything, with the rates of usury, and the accumulations of the compound interest.

Mme. Loisel looked old now. She had become the woman of impoverished households—strong and hard and rough. With frowsy hair, skirts askew, and red hands, she talked loud while washing the floor with great swishes of water. But sometimes, when her husband was at the office, she sat down near the window, and she thought of that gay evening of long ago, of that ball where she had been so beautiful and so fêted.

What would have happened if she had not lost that necklace? Who knows? Who knows? How life is strange and how changeful! How little a thing is needed for us to be lost or to be saved!

But, one Sunday, having gone to take a walk in the Champs Elysées to refresh herself from the labors of the week, she suddenly perceived a woman who was leading a child. It was Mme. Forestier, still young, still beautiful, still charming.

Mme. Loisel felt moved. Was she going to speak to her? Yes, certainly. And now that she had paid, she was going to tell her all about it. Why not?

She went up.

"Good-day, Jeanne."

The other, astonished to be familiarly addressed by this plain good wife, did not recognize her at all, and stammered:

"But—madame!—I do not know—You must have mistaken."

"No. I am Mathilde Loisel."

Her friend uttered a cry.

"Oh, my poor Mathilde! How you are changed!"

"Yes, I have had days hard enough, since I have seen you, days wretched enough—and that because of you!"

"Of me! How so?"

"Do you remember that diamond necklace which you lent me to wear at the ministerial ball?"

"Yes. Well?"

"Well, I lost it."

"What do you mean? You brought it back."

"I brought you back another just like it. And for this we have been ten years paying. You can understand that it was not easy for us, us who had nothing. At last it is ended, and I am very glad."

Mme. Forestier had stopped.

"You say that you bought a necklace of diamonds to replace mine?"

"Yes. You never noticed it, then! They were very like."

And she smiled with a joy which was proud and naïve at once.

Mme. Forestier, strongly moved, took her two hands.

"Oh, my poor Mathilde! Why, my necklace was paste. It was worth at most five hundred francs!"

That Holy Thing

by George MacDonald (1824-1905)

George MacDonald was a Scottish minister who became a writer and had a profound influence on C. S. Lewis.

They all were looking for a king
  To slay their foes, and lift them high:
Thou cam'st a little baby thing
  That made a woman cry.

O son of man, to right my lot
  Nought but thy presence can avail;
Yet on the road thy wheels are not,
  Nor on the sea thy sail!

My fancied ways why shouldst thou heed?
  Thou com'st down thine own secret stair:
Com'st down to answer all my need,
  Yea, every bygone prayer!

Where Love Is, God Is
by Leo Tolstoy (1885)

In a certain town there lived a cobbler, Martin Avdéiteh by name. He had a tiny room in a basement, the one window of which looked out on to the street. Through it one could only see the feet of those who passed by, but Martin recognized the people by their boots. He had lived long in the place and had many acquaintances. There was hardly a pair of boots in the neighbourhood that had not been once or twice through his hands, so he often saw his own handiwork through the window. Some he had re-soled, some patched, some stitched up, and to some he had even put fresh uppers. He had plenty to do, for he worked well, used good material, did not charge too much, and could be relied on. If he could do a job by the day required, he undertook it; if not, he told the truth and gave no false promises; so he was well known and never short of work.

Martin had always been a good man; but in his old age he began to think more about his soul and to draw nearer to God. While he still worked for a master, before he set up on his own account, his wife had died, leaving him with a three-year old son. None of his elder children had lived; they had all died in infancy. At first Martin thought of sending his little son to his sister's in the country, but then he felt sorry to part with the boy, thinking: 'It would be hard for my little Kapitón to have to grow up in a strange family; I will keep him with me.'

Martin left his master and went into lodgings with his little son. But he had no luck with his children. No sooner had the boy reached an age when he could help his father and be a support as well as a joy to him, than he fell ill and, after being laid up for a week with a burning fever, died. Martin buried his son, and gave way to despair so great and overwhelming that he murmured against God. In his sorrow he prayed again and again that he too might die, reproaching God for having taken the son he loved, his only son while he, old as he was, remained alive. After that Martin left off going to church.

One day an old man from Martin's native village who had been a pilgrim for the last eight years, called in on his way from Tróitsa Monastery. Martin opened his heart to him, and told him of his sorrow.

"I no longer even wish to live, holy man," he said. "All I ask of God is that I soon may die. I am now quite without hope in the world."

The old man replied: "You have no right to say such things, Martin. We cannot judge God's ways. Not our reasoning, but God's will, decides. If God willed that your son should die and you should live, it must be best so. As to your despair—that comes because you wish to live for your own happiness."

"What else should one live for?" asked Martin.

"For God, Martin," said the old man. "He gives you life, and you must live for Him. When you have learned to live for Him, you will grieve no more, and all will seem easy to you."

Martin was silent awhile, and then asked: "But how is one to live for God?"

The old man answered: "How one may live for God has been shown us by Christ. Can you read? Then buy the Gospels, and read them: there you will see how God would have you live. You have it all there."

These words sank deep into Martin's heart, and that same day he went and bought himself a Testament in large print, and began to read.

At first he meant only to read on holidays, but having once begun he found it made his heart so light that he read every day. Sometimes he was so absorbed in his reading that the oil in his lamp burnt out before he could tear himself away from the book. He continued to read every night, and the more he read the more clearly he understood what God required of him, and how he might live for God. And his heart grew lighter and lighter. Before, when he went to bed he used to lie with a heavy heart, moaning as he thought of his little Kapitón; but now he only repeated again and again: "Glory to Thee, glory to Thee, O Lord! Thy will be done!"

From that time Martin's whole life changed. Formerly, on holidays he used to go and have tea at the public house, and did not even refuse a glass or two of vódka. Sometimes, after having had a drop with a friend, he left the public house not drunk, but rather merry, and would say foolish things: shout at a man, or abuse him. Now, all that sort of thing passed away from him. His life became peaceful and joyful. He sat down to his work in the morning, and when he had finished his day's work he took the lamp down from the wall, stood it on the table, fetched his book from the shelf, opened it, and sat down to read. The more he read the better he understood, and the clearer and happier he felt in his mind.

It happened once that Martin sat up late, absorbed in his book. He was reading Luke's Gospel; and in the sixth chapter he came upon the verses:

"To him that smiteth thee on the one cheek offer also the other; and from him that taketh away thy cloak withhold not thy coat also. Give to every man that asketh thee; and of him that taketh away thy goods ask them not again. And as ye would that men should do to you, do ye also to them likewise."

He also read the verses where our Lord says:

"And why call ye me, Lord, Lord, and do not the things which I say? Whosoever cometh to me, and heareth my sayings, and doeth them, I will shew you to whom he is like: He is like a man which built an house, and digged deep, and laid the foundation on a rock: and when the flood arose, the stream beat vehemently upon that house, and could not shake it: for it was founded upon a rock. But he that heareth and doeth not, is like a man that without a foundation built an house upon the earth, against which the stream did beat vehemently, and immediately it fell; and the ruin of that house was great."

When Martin read these words his soul was glad within him. He took off his spectacles and laid them on the book, and leaning his elbows on the table pondered over what he had read. He tried his own life by the standard of those words, asking himself:

"Is my house built on the rock, or on sand? If it stands on the rock, it is well. It seems easy enough while one sits here alone, and one thinks one has done all that God commands; but as soon as I cease to be on my guard, I sin again. Still I will persevere. It brings such joy. Help me, O Lord!"

He thought all this, and was about to go to bed, but was loath to leave his book. So he went on reading the seventh chapter—about the centurion, the widow's son, and the answer to John's disciples—and he came to the part where a rich Pharisee invited the Lord to his house; and he read how the woman who was a sinner, anointed his feet and washed them with her tears, and how he justified her. Coming to the forty-fourth verse, he read:

"And turning to the woman, he said unto Simon, Seest thou this woman? I entered into thine house. Thou gavest me no water for my feet: but she hath wetted my feet with her tears, and wiped them with her hair. Thou gavest me no kiss; but she, since the time I came in, hath not ceased to kiss my feet. My head with oil thou didst not anoint: but she hath anointed my feet with ointment."

He read these verses and thought: "He gave no water for his feet, gave no kiss, his head with oil he did not anoint. . . ." And Martin took off his spectacles once more, laid them on his book, and pondered.

"He must have been like me, that Pharisee. He too thought only of himself—how to get a cup of tea, how to keep warm and comfortable; never a thought of his guest. He took care of himself, but for his guest he cared nothing at all. Yet who was the guest? The Lord himself! If he came to me, should I behave like that?"

Then Martin laid his head upon both his arms and, before he was aware of it, he fell asleep.

"Martin!" he suddenly heard a voice, as if some one had breathed the word above his ear.

He started from his sleep. "Who's there?" he asked.

He turned round and looked at the door; no one was there. He called again. Then he heard quite distinctly: "Martin, Martin! Look out into the street tomorrow, for I shall come."

Martin roused himself, rose from his chair and rubbed his eyes, but did not know whether he had heard these words in a dream or awake. He put out the lamp and lay down to sleep.

Next morning he rose before daylight, and after saying his prayers he lit the fire and prepared his cabbage soup and buckwheat porridge. Then he lit the samovár, put on his apron, and sat down by the window to his work. As he sat working Martin thought over what had happened the night before. At times it seemed to him like a dream, and at times he thought that he had really heard the voice. "Such things have happened before now," thought he.

So he sat by the window, looking out into the street more than he worked, and whenever any one passed in unfamiliar boots he would stoop and look up, so as to see not the feet only but the face of the passer-by as well. A house-porter passed in new felt boots; then a water-carrier. Presently an old soldier of Nicholas' reign came near the window, spade in hand. Martin knew him by his boots, which were shabby old felt ones, galoshed with leather. The old man was called Stepánitch: a neighbouring tradesman kept him in his house for charity, and his duty was to help the house-porter. He began to clear away the snow before Martin's window. Martin glanced at him and then went on with his work.

"I must be growing crazy with age," said Martin, laughing at his fancy. "Stepánitch comes to clear away the snow, and I must needs imagine it's Christ coming to visit me. Old dotard that I am!"

Yet after he had made a dozen stitches he felt drawn to look out of the window again. He saw that Stepánitch had leaned his spade against the wall, and was either resting himself or trying to get warm. The man was old and broken down, and had evidently not enough strength even to clear away the snow.

"What if I called him in and gave him some tea?" thought Martin. "The samovár is just on the boil."

He stuck his awl in its place, and rose; and putting the samovár on the table, made tea. Then he tapped the window with his fingers. Stepánitch turned and came to the window. Martin beckoned to him to come in, and went himself to open the door.

"Come in," he said, "and warm yourself a bit. I'm sure you must be cold."

"May God bless you!" Stepánitch answered. "My bones do ache to be sure." He came in, first shaking off the snow, and lest he should leave marks on the floor he began wiping his feet; but as he did so he tottered and nearly fell.

"Don't trouble to wipe your feet," said Martin. "I'll wipe up the floor—it's all in the day's work. Come, friend, sit down and have some tea."

Filling two tumblers, he passed one to his visitor, and pouring his own out into the saucer, began to blow on it.

Stepánitch emptied his glass, and, turning it upside down, put the remains of his piece of sugar on the top. He began to express his thanks, but it was plain that he would be glad of some more.

"Have another glass," said Martin, refilling the visitor's tumbler and his own. But while he drank his tea Martin kept looking out into the street.

"Are you expecting any one?" asked the visitor.

"Am I expecting any one? Well, now, I'm ashamed to tell you. It isn't that I really expect any one; but I heard something last night which I can't get out of my mind. Whether it was a vision, or only a fancy, I can't tell. You see, friend, last night I was

reading the Gospel, about Christ the Lord, how he suffered, and how he walked on earth. You have heard tell of it, I dare say."

"I have heard tell of it," answered Stepánitch; "but I'm an ignorant man and not able to read."

"Well, you see, I was reading of how he walked on earth. I came to that part, you know, where he went to a Pharisee who did not receive him well. Well, friend, as I read about it, I thought how that man did not receive Christ the Lord with proper honour. Suppose such a thing could happen to such a man as myself, I thought, what would I not do to receive him! But that man gave him no reception at all. Well, friend, as I was thinking of this, I began to doze, and as I dozed I heard some one call me by name. I got up, and thought I heard someone whispering, 'Expect me; I will come tomorrow.' This happened twice over. And to tell you the truth, it sank so into my mind that, though I am ashamed of it myself, I keep on expecting him, the dear Lord!"

Stepánitch shook his head in silence, finished his tumbler and laid it on its side; but Martin stood it up again and refilled it for him.

"Here drink another glass, bless you! And I was thinking too, how he walked on earth and despised no one, but went mostly among common folk. He went with plain people, and chose his disciples from among the likes of us, from workmen like us, sinners that we are. 'He who raises himself,' he said, 'shall be humbled and he who humbles himself shall be raised.' 'You call me Lord,' he said, 'and I will wash your feet.' 'He who would be first,' he said, 'let him be the servant of all; because,' he said, 'blessed are the poor, the humble, the meek, and the merciful.'"

Stepánitch forgot his tea. He was an old man easily moved to tears, and as he sat and listened the tears ran down his cheeks.

"Come, drink some more," said Martin. But Stepánitch crossed himself, thanked him, moved away his tumbler, and rose.

"Thank you, Martin Avdéitch," he said, "you have given me food and comfort both for soul and body."

"You're very welcome. Come again another time. I am glad to have a guest," said Martin.

Stepánitch went away; and Martin poured out the last of the tea and drank it up. Then he put away the tea things and sat down to his work, stitching the back seam of a boot. And as he stitched he kept looking out of the window, waiting for Christ, and thinking about him and his doings. And his head was full of Christ's sayings.

Two soldiers went by: one in government boots the other in boots of his own; then the master of a neighbouring house, in shining galoshes; then a baker carrying a basket. All these passed on. Then a woman came up in worsted stockings and peasant-made shoes. She passed the window, but stopped by the wall. Martin glanced up at her through the window, and saw that she was a stranger, poorly dressed, and with a baby in her arms. She stopped by the wall with her back to the wind, trying to wrap the baby up though she had hardly anything to wrap it in. The woman had only summer clothes on, and even they were shabby and worn. Through the window Martin heard the baby crying, and the woman trying to soothe it, but unable to do so. Martin rose and, going out of the door and up the steps, he called to her.

"My dear, I say, my dear!"

The woman heard, and turned round.

"Why do you stand out there with the baby in the cold? Come inside. You can wrap him up better in a warm place. Come this way!"

The woman was surprised to see an old man in an apron, with spectacles on his nose, calling to her, but she followed him in.

They went down the steps, entered the little room, and the old man led her to the bed.

"There, sit down, my dear, near the stove. Warm yourself, and feed the baby."

"Haven't any milk. I have eaten nothing myself since early morning," said the woman, but still she took the baby to her breast.

Martin shook his head. He brought out a basin and some bread. Then he opened the oven door and poured some cabbage soup into the basin. He took out the porridge pot also but the porridge was not yet ready, so he spread a cloth on the table and served only the soup and bread.

"Sit down and eat, my dear, and I'll mind the baby. Why, bless me, I've had children of my own; I know how to manage them."

The woman crossed herself, and sitting down at the table began to eat, while Martin put the baby on the bed and sat down by it. He chucked and chucked, but having no teeth he could not do it well and the baby continued to cry. Then Martin tried poking at him with his finger; he drove his finger straight at the baby's mouth and then quickly drew it back, and did this again and again. He did not let the baby take his finger in its mouth, because it was all black with cobbler's wax. But the baby first grew quiet watching the finger, and then began to laugh. And Martin felt quite pleased.

The woman sat eating and talking, and told him who she was, and where she had been.

"I'm a soldier's wife," said she. "They sent my husband somewhere, far away, eight months ago, and I have heard nothing of him since. I had a place as cook till my baby was born, but then they would not keep me with a child. For three months now I have been struggling, unable to find a place, and I've had to sell all I had for food. I tried to go as a wet-nurse, but no one would have me; they said I was too starved-looking and thin. Now I have just been to see a tradesman's wife (a woman from our village is in service with her) and she has promised to take me. I thought it was all settled at last, but she tells me not to come till next week. It is far to her place, and I am fagged out, and baby is quite starved, poor mite. Fortunately our landlady has pity on us, and lets us lodge free, else I don't know what we should do."

Martin sighed. "Haven't you any warmer clothing?" he asked.

"How could I get warm clothing?" said she. "Why I pawned my last shawl for sixpence yesterday."

Then the woman came and took the child, and Martin got up. He went and looked among some things that were hanging on the wall, and brought back an old cloak.

"Here," he said, "though it's a worn-out old thing, it will do to wrap him up in."

The woman looked at the cloak, then at the old man, and taking it, burst into tears. Martin turned away, and groping under the bed brought out a small trunk. He fumbled about in it, and again sat down opposite the woman. And the woman said:

"The Lord bless you, friend. Surely Christ must have sent me to your window, else the child would have frozen. It was mild when I started, but now see how cold it has turned. Surely it must have been Christ who made you look out of your window and take pity on me, poor wretch!"

Martin smiled and said, "It is quite true; it was he made me do it. It was no mere chance made me look out."

And he told the woman his dream, and how he had heard the Lord's voice promising to visit him that day.

"Who knows? All things are possible," said the woman. And she got up and threw the cloak over her shoulders, wrapping it round herself and round the baby. Then she bowed, and thanked Martin once more.

"Take this for Christ's sake," said Martin, and gave her sixpence to get her shawl out of pawn. The woman crossed herself, and Martin did the same, and then he saw her out.

After the woman had gone, Martin ate some cabbage soup, cleared the things away, and sat down to work again. He sat and worked, but did not forget the window, and every time a shadow fell on it he looked up at once to see who was passing. People he knew and strangers passed by, but no one remarkable.

After a while Martin saw an apple-woman stop just in front of his window. She had a large basket, but there did not seem to be many apples left in it; she had evidently sold most of her stock. On her back she had a sack full of chips, which she was taking home. No doubt she had gathered them at some place where building was going on. The sack evidently hurt her, and she wanted to shift it from one shoulder to the other, so she put it down on the footpath and, placing her basket on a post, began to shake down the chips in the sack. While she was doing this a boy in a tattered cap ran up, snatched an apple out of the basket, and tried to slip away; but the old woman noticed it, and turning, caught the boy by his sleeve. He began to struggle, trying to free himself, but the old woman held on with both hands, knocked his cap off his head, and seized hold of his hair. The boy screamed and the old woman scolded. Martin dropped his awl, not waiting to stick it in its place, and rushed out of the door. Stumbling up the steps, and dropping his spectacles in his hurry, he ran out into the street. The old woman was pulling the boy's hair and scolding him, and threatening to take him to the police. The lad was struggling and protesting, saying, "I did not take it. What are you beating me for? Let me go!"

Martin separated them. He took the boy by the hand and said, "Let him go, Granny. Forgive him for Christ's sake."

"I'll pay him out, so that he won't forget it for a year! I'll take the rascal to the police!"

Martin began entreating the old woman.

"Let him go, Granny. He won't do it again. Let him go for Christ's sake!"

The old woman let go, and the boy wished to run away, but Martin stopped him.

"Ask the Granny's forgiveness!" said he. "And don't do it another time. I saw you take the apple."

The boy began to cry and to beg pardon.

"That's right. And now here's an apple for you, and Martin took an apple from the basket and gave it to the boy, saying, "I will pay you, Granny."

"You will spoil them that way, the young rascals," said the old woman. "He ought to be whipped so that he should remember it for a week."

"Oh, Granny, Granny," said Martin, "that's our way—but it's not God's way. If he should be whipped for stealing an apple, what should be done to us for our sins?"

The old woman was silent.

And Martin told her the parable of the lord who forgave his servant a large debt, and how the servant went out and seized his debtor by the throat. The old woman listened to it all, and the boy, too, stood by and listened.

"God bids us forgive," said Martin, "or else we shall not be forgiven. Forgive every one; and a thoughtless youngster most of all."

The old woman wagged her head and sighed.

"It's true enough," said she, "but they are getting terribly spoiled."

"Then we old ones must show them better ways," Martin replied.

"That's just what I say," said the old woman. "I have had seven of them myself, and only one daughter is left." And the old woman began to tell how and where she was living with her daughter, and how many grandchildren she had. "There now," she said, "I have but little strength left, yet I work hard for the sake of my grandchildren; and nice children they are, too. No one comes out to meet me but the children. Little Annie, now, won't leave me for any one. It's 'grandmother, dear grandmother, darling grandmother.'" And the old woman completely softened at the thought.

"Of course, it was only his childishness, God help him," said she, referring to the boy.

As the old woman was about to hoist her sack on her back, the lad sprang forward to her, saying, "Let me carry it for you, Granny. I'm going that way."

The old woman nodded her head, and put the sack on the boy's back, and they went down the street together, the old woman quite forgetting to ask Martin to pay for the apple. Martin stood and watched them as they went along talking to each other.

When they were out of sight Martin went back to the house. Having found his spectacles unbroken on the steps, he picked up his awl and sat down again to work. He worked a little, but could soon not see to pass the bristle through the holes in the leather; and presently he noticed the lamplighter passing on his way to light the street lamps.

"Seems it's time to light up," thought he. So he trimmed his lamp, hung it up, and sat down again to work. He finished off one boot and, turning it about, examined it. It was all right. Then he gathered his tools together, swept up the cuttings, put away the bristles and the thread and the awls, and, taking down the lamp, placed it on the table. Then he took the Gospels from the shelf. He meant to open them at the place he had marked the day before with a bit of morocco, but the book opened at another place. As Martin opened it, his yesterday's dream came back to his mind, and no sooner had he thought of it than he seemed to hear footsteps, as though some one were moving behind him. Martin turned round, and it seemed to him as if people were standing in the dark corner, but he could not make out who they were. And a voice whispered in his ear: "Martin, Martin, don't you know me?"

"Who is it?" muttered Martin.

"It is I," said the voice. And out of the dark corner stepped Stepánitch, who smiled and vanishing like a cloud was seen no more.

"It is I," said the voice again. And out of the darkness stepped the woman with the baby in her arms and the woman smiled and the baby laughed, and they too vanished.

"It is I," said the voice once more. And the old woman and the boy with the apple stepped out and both smiled, and then they too vanished.

And Martin's soul grew glad. He crossed himself, put on his spectacles, and began reading the Gospel just where it had opened; and at the top of the page he read:

"I was an hungered, and ye gave me meat: I was thirsty, and ye gave me drink: I was a stranger, and ye took me in."

And at the bottom of the page he read:

"Inasmuch as ye did it unto one of these my brethren even these least, ye did it unto me" (Matt. xxv).

And Martin understood that his dream had come true; and that the Saviour had really come to him that day, and he had welcomed him.

Crossing the Bar
by Alfred, Lord Tennyson (1889)

One of Tennyson's most famous quotations is this: "More things are wrought by prayer in this world than this world dreams of." He asked that this poem always be placed last in anthologies of his works.

Sunset and evening star,
And one clear call for me!
And may there be no moaning of the bar
When I put out to sea.

But such a tide as moving seems asleep,
Too full for sound and foam.
When that which drew from the boundless deep
Turns again home.

Twilight and evening bell,
And after that the dark!
And may there be no sadness of farewell
When I embark.

For, though from out our bourne of time and place
The flood may bear me far,
I hope to see my Pilot face to face
When I have crossed the bar.

Alfred, Lord Tennyson

If – by Rudyard Kipling (1895)

Rudyard Kipling (1865-1936) was born in India and became the voice for British colonialism in the late Victorian era through his poetry, short stories, and books. He was the first Englishman to receive the Nobel Prize in literature (1907). He died January 18, 1936 in London and was buried in Westminster Abbey. This poem was published in Rewards *and* Fairies, *a 1910 collection of poems and short stories.*

 f you can keep your head when all about you
Are losing theirs and blaming it on you;
If you can trust yourself when all men doubt you,
But make allowance for their doubting too;
If you can wait and not be tired by waiting,
Or being lied about, don't deal in lies,
Or being hated, don't give way to hating,
And yet don't look too good, nor talk too wise;

If you can dream—and not make dreams your master;
If you can think—and not make thoughts your aim,
If you can meet with Triumph and Disaster
And treat those two impostors just the same;
If you can bear to hear the truth you've spoken
Twisted by knaves to make a trap for fools,
Or watch the things you gave your life to, broken,
And stoop and build 'em up with worn-out tools;

If you can make one heap of all your winnings
And risk it on one turn of pitch-and-toss,
And lose, and start again at your beginnings
And never breathe a word about your loss;
If you can force your heart and nerve and sinew
To serve your turn long after they are gone,
And so hold on when there is nothing in you
Except the Will which says to them: 'Hold on!'

If you can talk with crowds and keep your virtue,
Or walk with Kings—nor lose the common touch,
If neither foes nor loving friends can hurt you,
If all men count with you, but none too much;
If you can fill the unforgiving minute
With sixty seconds' worth of distance run,
Yours is the Earth and everything that's in it,
And—which is more—you'll be a Man, my son!

Father in Heaven, Who Lovest All
by Rudyard Kipling (1906)

Father in heaven, Who lovest all,
O help Thy children when they call,
That they may build from age to age
An undefiled heritage.

Teach us to bear the yoke in youth,
With steadfastness and careful truth,
That, in our time, Thy grace may give
The truth whereby the nations live.

Teach us to rule ourselves alway,
Controlled and cleanly night and day,
That we may bring, if need arise,
No maimed or worthless sacrifice.

Teach us to look in all our ends,
On Thee for Judge, and not our friends,
That we, with Thee, may walk uncowed
By fear or favor of the crowd.

Teach us the strength that cannot seek,
By deed or thought, to hurt the weak,
That, under Thee, we may possess
Man's strength to comfort man's distress.

Teach us delight in simple things,
And mirth that has no bitter springs,
Forgiveness free of evil done,
And love to all men 'neath the sun.

Rudyard Kipling

Requiem

by Robert Louis Stevenson (1913)

Robert Louis Stevenson (1850-1894) suffered from tuberculosis most of his life and traveled extensively to find relief. He wrote a wide variety of poems, stories, and novels that remain popular today.

Under the wide and starry sky,
Dig the grave and let me lie.
Glad did I live and gladly die,
And I laid me down with a will.

This be the verse you grave for me:
Here he lies where he longed to be;
Home is the sailor, home from sea,
And the hunter home from the hill.

Robert Louis Stevenson

Pied Beauty

by Gerard Manley Hopkins (1918)

Gerard Manley Hopkins (1844-1889) was an English Jesuit priest whose poems were not published during his lifetime by his own request. He often used innovative rhythms and phrasing that challenge readers.

> Glory be to God for dappled things —
> For skies of couple-colour as a brinded cow;
> For rose-moles all in stipple upon trout that swim;
> Fresh-firecoal chestnut-falls; finches' wings;
> Landscape plotted and pieced — fold, fallow, and plough;
> And áll trádes, their gear and tackle and trim.
>
> All things counter, original, spare, strange;
> Whatever is fickle, freckled (who knows how?)
> With swift, slow; sweet, sour; adazzle, dim;
> He fathers-forth whose beauty is past change:
> Praise him.

Iron Curtain Speech
by Winston Churchill (1946)

Presented at Westminster College, Fulton, Missouri, March 5, 1946

Churchill was introduced for this speech by President Harry S. Truman, who is pictured here with Josef Stalin, Premier of the U.S.S.R.
Left Front: Truman;
Right Front: Stalin

President McCluer, ladies and gentlemen, and last, but certainly not least, the President of the United States of America:

I am very glad indeed to come to Westminster College this afternoon, and I am complimented that you should give me a degree from an institution whose reputation has been so solidly established. The name "Westminster" somehow or other seems familiar to me. I feel as if I have heard of it before. Indeed now that I come to think of it, it was at Westminster that I received a very large part of my education in politics, dialectic, rhetoric, and one or two other things. In fact we have both been educated at the same, or similar, or, at any rate, kindred establishments.

It is also an honor, ladies and gentlemen, perhaps almost unique, for a private visitor to be introduced to an academic audience by the President of the United States. Amid his heavy burdens, duties, and responsibilities—unsought but not recoiled from—the President has traveled a thousand miles to dignify and magnify our meeting here to-day and to give me an opportunity of addressing this kindred nation, as well as my own countrymen across the ocean, and perhaps some other countries too. The President has told you that it is his wish, as I am sure it is yours, that I should have full liberty to give my true and faithful counsel in these anxious and baffling times. I shall certainly avail myself of this freedom, and feel the more right to do so because any private ambitions I may have cherished in my younger days have been satisfied beyond my wildest dreams. Let me however make it clear that I have no official mission or status of any kind, and that I speak only for myself. There is nothing here but what you see.

I can therefore allow my mind, with the experience of a lifetime, to play over the problems which beset us on the morrow of our absolute victory in arms, and to try to make sure with what strength I have that what has been gained with so much sacrifice and suffering shall be preserved for the future glory and safety of mankind.

Ladies and gentlemen, the United States stands at this time at the pinnacle of world power. It is a solemn moment for the American Democracy. For with primacy in power is also joined an awe-inspiring accountability to the future. If you look around you, you must feel not only the sense of duty done but also you must feel anxiety lest you fall below the level of achievement. Opportunity is here and now, clear and shining for both our countries. To reject it or ignore it or fritter it away will bring upon us all the long reproaches of the after-time. It is necessary that the constancy of mind, persistency of purpose, and the grand simplicity of decision shall rule and guide the conduct of the English-speaking peoples in peace as they did in war. We must, and I believe we shall, prove ourselves equal to this severe requirement.

President McCluer, when American military men approach some serious situation they are wont to write at the head of their directive the words "over-all strategic concept". There is wisdom in this, as it leads to clarity of thought. What then is the over-all strategic concept which we should inscribe today? It is nothing less than the safety and welfare, the freedom and progress, of all the homes and families of all the men and women in all the lands. And here I speak particularly of the myriad cottage or apartment homes where the wage-earner strives

*Prime Minister Churchill
in Quebec, 1943*

amid the accidents and difficulties of life to guard his wife and children from privation and bring the family up in the fear of the Lord, or upon ethical conceptions which often play their potent part.

To give security to these countless homes, they must be shielded form two gaunt marauders, war and tyranny. We all know the frightful disturbance in which the ordinary family is plunged when the curse of war swoops down upon the bread-winner and those for whom he works and contrives. The awful ruin of Europe, with all its vanished glories, and of large parts of Asia glares us in the eyes. When the designs of wicked men or the aggressive urge of mighty States dissolve over large areas the frame of civilized society, humble folk are confronted with difficulties with which they cannot cope. For them all is distorted, all is broken, all is even ground to pulp.

When I stand here this quiet afternoon I shudder to visualize what is actually happening to millions now and what is going to happen in this period when famine stalks the earth. None can compute what has been called "the unestimated sum of human pain." Our supreme task and duty is to guard the homes of the common people from the horrors and miseries of another war. We are all agreed on that.

Our American military colleagues, after having proclaimed their "over-all strategic concept" and computed available resources, always proceed to the next step—namely, the method. Here again there is widespread agreement. A world organization has already been erected for the prime purpose of preventing war. UNO, the successor of the League of Nations, with the decisive addition of the United States and all that that means, is already at work. We must make sure that its work is fruitful, that it is a reality and not a sham, that it is a force for action, and not merely a frothing of words, that it is a true temple of peace in which the shields of many nations can some day be hung up, and not merely a cockpit in a Tower of Babel. Before we cast away the solid assurances of national armaments for self-preservation we must be certain that our temple is built, not upon shifting sands or quagmires, but upon a rock. Anyone can see with his eyes open that our path will be difficult and also long, but if we persevere together as we did in the two world wars—though not, alas, in the interval between them—I cannot doubt that we shall achieve our common purpose in the end.

I have, however, a definite and practical proposal to make for action. Courts and magistrates may be set up but they cannot function without sheriffs and constables. The United Nations Organization must immediately begin to be equipped with an international armed force. In such a matter we can only go step by step, but we must begin now. I propose that each of the Powers and States should be invited to dedicate a certain number of air

Prime Minister Churchill (right) in Quebec, 1943

squadrons to the service of the world organization. These squadrons would be trained and prepared in their own countries, but would move around in rotation from one country to another. They would wear the uniforms of their own countries but with different badges. They would not be required to act against their own nation, but in other respects they would be directed by the world organization. This might be started on a modest scale and it would grow as confidence grew. I wished to see this done after the first world war, and I devoutly trust that it may be done forthwith.

It would nevertheless, ladies and gentlemen, be wrong and imprudent to entrust the secret knowledge or experience of the atomic bomb, which the United States, Great Britain, and Canada now share, to the world organization, while still in its infancy. It would be criminal madness to cast it adrift in this still agitated and un-united world. No one country has slept less well in their beds because this knowledge and the method and the raw materials to apply it, are at present largely retained in American hands. I do not believe we should all have slept so soundly had the positions been reversed and some Communist or neo-Fascist State monopolized for the time being these dread agencies. The fear of them alone might easily have been used to enforce totalitarian systems upon the free democratic world, with consequences appalling to human imagination. God has willed that this shall not be and we have at least a breathing space to set our world house in order before this peril has to be encountered: and even then, if no effort is spared, we should still possess so formidable a superiority as to impose effective deterrents upon its employment, or threat of employment, by others. Ultimately, when the essential brotherhood of man is truly embodied and expressed in a world organization with all the necessary practical safeguards to make it effective, these powers would naturally be confided to that world organization.

Now I come to the second of the two marauders, to the second danger which threatens the cottage homes, and the ordinary people—namely, tyranny. We cannot be blind to the fact that the liberties enjoyed by individual citizens throughout the United States and throughout the British Empire are not valid in a considerable number of countries, some of which are very powerful. In these States control is enforced upon the common people by various kinds of all-embracing police governments to a degree which is overwhelming and contrary to every principle of democracy. The power of the State is exercised without restraint, either by dictators or by compact oligarchies operating through a privileged party and a political police. It is not our duty at this time when difficulties are so numerous to interfere forcibly in the internal affairs of countries which we have not conquered in war. But we must never cease

*Prime Minister Churchill
in Quebec, 1943*

to proclaim in fearless tones the great principles of freedom and the rights of man which are the joint inheritance of the English-speaking world and which through Magna Carta, the Bill of rights, the Habeas Corpus, trial by jury, and the English common law find their most famous expression in the American Declaration of Independence.

All this means that the people of any country have the right, and should have the power by constitutional action, by free unfettered elections, with secret ballot, to choose or change the character or form of government under which they dwell; that freedom of speech and thought should reign; that courts of justice, independent of the executive, unbiased by any party, should administer laws which have received the broad assent of large majorities or are consecrated by time and custom. Here are the title deeds of freedom which should lie in every cottage home. Here is the message of the British and American peoples to mankind. Let us preach what we practice—let us practice what we preach.

Though I have now stated the two great dangers which menace the home of the people, War and Tyranny, I have not yet spoken of poverty and privation which are in many cases the prevailing anxiety. But if the dangers of war and tyranny are removed, there is no doubt that science and cooperation can bring in the next few years, certainly in the next few decades, to the world, newly taught in the sharpening school of war, an expansion of material well-being beyond anything that has yet occurred in human experience.

Now, at this sad and breathless moment, we are plunged in the hunger and distress which are the aftermath of our stupendous struggle; but this will pass and may pass quickly, and there is no reason except human folly or sub-human crime which should deny to all the nations the inauguration and enjoyment of an age of plenty. I have often used words which I learned fifty years ago from a great Irish-American orator, a friend of mine, Mr. Bourke Cockran, "There is enough for all. The earth is a generous mother; she will provide in plentiful abundance food for all her children if they will but cultivate her soil in justice and peace." So far I feel that we are in full agreement.

Prime Minister Churchill in Quebec, 1944

Now, while still pursing the method—the method of realizing our over-all strategic concept, I come to the crux of what I have traveled here to say. Neither the sure prevention of war, nor the continuous rise of world organization will be gained without what I have called the fraternal association of the English-speaking peoples. This means a special relationship between the British Commonwealth and Empire and the United States of America. Ladies and gentlemen, this is no time for generality, and I will venture to the precise. Fraternal association requires not only the growing friendship and mutual understanding between our two vast but kindred systems of society, but the continuance of the intimate relations between our military advisers, leading to common study of potential dangers, the similarity of weapons and manuals of instructions, and to the interchange of officers and cadets at technical colleges. It should carry with it the continuance of the present facilities for mutual security by the joint use of all Naval and Air Force bases in the possession of either country all over the world. This would perhaps double the mobility of the American Navy and Air Force. It would greatly expand that of the British Empire forces and it might well lead, if and as the world calms down, to important financial savings. Already we use together a large number of islands; more may well be entrusted to our joint care in the near future.

The United States has already a Permanent Defense Agreement with the Dominion of Canada, which is so devotedly attached to the British Commonwealth and the Empire. This Agreement is more effective than many of those which have been made under formal alliances. This principle should be extended to all the British Commonwealths with full reciprocity. Thus, whatever happens, and thus only, shall we be secure ourselves and able to work together for the high and simple causes that are dear to us and bode no ill to any. Eventually there may come—I feel eventually there will come—the principle of common citizenship, but that we may be content to leave to destiny, whose outstretched arm many of us can already clearly see.

There is however an important question we must ask ourselves. Would a special relationship between the United States and the British Commonwealth be inconsistent with our over-riding loyalties to the World Organization? I reply that, on the contrary, it is probably the only means by which that organization will achieve its full stature and strength. There are already the special United States relations with Canada that I have just mentioned, and there are the relations between the United States and the South American Republics. We British have also our twenty years Treaty of Collaboration and Mutual Assistance with Soviet Russia. I agree with Mr. Bevin, the Foreign Secretary of Great Britain, that it might well be a fifty years treaty so far as we are concerned. We aim at nothing but mutual assistance and collaboration with Russia. The British have an alliance with Portugal unbroken since the year 1384, and which produced fruitful results at a critical moment in the recent war. None of these clash with the general interest of a world agreement, or a world organization; on the contrary, they help it. "In my father's house are many mansions." Special associations between members of the United Nations which have no aggressive point against any other country, which harbor no design incompatible with the Charter of the United Nations, far from being harmful, are beneficial and, as I believe, indispensable.

Prime Minister Churchill (seated left) in Quebec, 1944

I spoke earlier, ladies and gentlemen, of the Temple of Peace. Workmen from all countries must build that temple. If two of the workmen know each other particularly well and are old friends, if their families are intermingled, if they have "faith in each other's purpose, hope in each other's future and charity towards each other's shortcomings"—to quote some good words I read here the other day—why cannot they work together at the common task as friends and partners? Why can they not share their tools and thus increase each other's working powers? Indeed they must do so or else the temple may not be built, or, being built, it may collapse, and we should all be proved again unteachable and have to go and try to learn again for a third time in a school of war incomparably more rigorous than that from which we have just been released. The dark ages may return, the Stone Age may return on the gleaming wings of science, and what might now shower immeasurable material blessings upon mankind, may even bring about its total destruction. Beware, I say; time may be short. Do not let us take the course of allowing events to drift along until it is too late. If there is to be a fraternal association of the kind I have described, with all the strength and security which both our countries can derive from it, let us make sure that that great fact is known to the world, and that it plays its part in steadying and stabilizing the foundations of peace. There is the path of wisdom. Prevention is better than the cure.

Communist Symbol

A shadow has fallen upon the scenes so lately light by the Allied victory. Nobody knows what Soviet Russia and its Communist international organization intends to do in the immediate future, or what are the limits, if any, to their expansive and proselytizing tendencies. I have a strong admiration and regard for the valiant Russian people and for my wartime comrade, Marshall Stalin. There is deep sympathy and goodwill in Britain—and I doubt not here also—towards the peoples of all the Russias and a resolve to persevere through many differences and rebuffs in establishing lasting friendships. We understand the Russian need to be secure on her western frontiers by the removal of all possibility of German aggression. We welcome Russia to her rightful place among the leading nations of the world. We welcome her flag upon the seas. Above all, we welcome, or should welcome, constant, frequent and growing contacts between the Russian people and our own people on both sides of the Atlantic. It is my duty however, for I am sure you would wish me to state the facts as I see them to you. It is my duty to place before you certain facts about the present position in Europe.

From Stettin in the Baltic to Trieste in the Adriatic an iron curtain has descended across the Continent. Behind that line lie all the capitals of the ancient states of Central and Eastern Europe. Warsaw, Berlin, Prague, Vienna, Budapest, Belgrade, Bucharest and Sofia, all these famous cities and the populations around them lie in what I must call the Soviet sphere, and all are subject in one form or another, not only to Soviet influence but to a very high and, in some cases, increasing measure of control from Moscow. Athens alone—Greece with its immortal glories—is free to decide its future at an election under British, American and French observation. The Russian-dominated Polish Government has been encouraged to make enormous and wrongful inroads upon Germany, and mass expulsions of millions of Germans on a scale grievous and undreamed-of are now taking place. The Communist parties, which were very small in all these Eastern States of Europe, have been raised to pre-eminence and power far beyond their numbers and are seeking everywhere to obtain totalitarian control. Police governments are prevailing in nearly every case, and so far, except in Czechoslovakia, there is no true democracy.

Turkey and Persia are both profoundly alarmed and disturbed at the claims which are being made upon them and at the pressure being exerted by the Moscow Government. An attempt is being made by the Russians in Berlin to build up a quasi-Communist party in their zone of occupied Germany by showing special favors to groups of left-wing German leaders. At the end of the fighting last June, the American and British Armies withdrew westward, in accordance with an earlier agreement, to a depth at some points of 150 miles upon a front of nearly four hundred miles, in order to allow our Russian allies to occupy this vast expanse of territory which the Western Democracies had conquered.

If now the Soviet Government tries, by separate action, to build up a pro-Communist Germany in their areas, this will cause new serious difficulties in the American and British zones, and will give the defeated Germans the power of putting themselves up to auction between the Soviets and the Western Democracies. Whatever conclusions may be drawn from these facts—and facts they are—this is certainly not the Liberated Europe we fought to build up. Nor is it one which contains the essentials of permanent peace.

The safety of the world, ladies and gentlemen, requires a new unity in Europe, from which no nation should be permanently outcast. It is from the quarrels of the strong parent races in Europe that the world wars we have witnessed, or which occurred in former times, have sprung. Twice in our own lifetime we have seen the United States, against their wishes and their traditions, against arguments, the force of which it is impossible not to comprehend, twice we have seen them drawn by irresistible forces, into these wars in time to secure the victory of the good cause, but only after frightful slaughter and devastation have occurred. Twice the United States has had to send several millions of its young men across the Atlantic to find the war; but now war can find any nation, wherever it may dwell between dusk and dawn. Surely we should work with conscious purpose for a grand pacification of Europe, within the structure of the United Nations and in accordance with our Charter. That I feel opens a course of policy of very great importance.

In front of the iron curtain which lies across Europe are other causes for anxiety. In Italy the Communist Party is seriously hampered by having to support the Communist-trained Marshal Tito's claims to former Italian territory at the head of the Adriatic. Nevertheless the future of Italy hangs in the balance. Again one cannot imagine a regenerated Europe without a strong France. All my public life I worked for a strong France, and I never lost faith in her destiny, even in the darkest hours. I will not lose faith now. However, in a great number of countries, far from the Russian frontiers and throughout the world, Communist fifth columns are established and work in complete unity and absolute obedience to the directions they receive from the Communist center. Except in the British Commonwealth and in the United States where Communism is in its infancy, the Communist parties or fifth columns constitute a growing challenge and peril to Christian civilization. These are somber facts for anyone to have recited on the morrow of a victory gained by so much splendid comradeship in arms and in the cause of freedom and democracy; but we should be most unwise not to face them squarely while time remains.

The outlook is also anxious in the Far East and especially in Manchuria. The Agreement which was made at Yalta, to which I was a party, was extremely favorable to Soviet Russia, but it was made at a time when no one could say that the German war might not extend all through the summer and autumn of 1945 and when the Japanese war was expected by the best judges to last for a further 18 months from the end of the German war.

Josef Stalin, Franklin Roosevelt, Winston Churchill, and others in Tehran, Iran, November 29, 1943

In this country you are all so well-informed about the Far East, and such devoted friends of China, that I do not need to expatiate on the situation there.

I have, however, felt bound to portray the shadow which, alike in the west and in the east, falls upon the world. I was a minister at the time of the Versailles treaty and a close friend of Mr. Lloyd-George, who was the head of the British delegation at Versailles. I did not myself agree with many things that were done, but I have a very strong impression in my mind of that situation, and I find it painful to contrast it with that which prevails now. In those days there were high hopes and unbounded confidence that the wars were over and that the League of Nations would become all-powerful. I do not see or feel that same confidence or even the same hopes in the haggard world at the present time.

On the other hand, ladies and gentlemen, I repulse the idea that a new war is inevitable; still more that it is imminent. It is because I am sure that our fortunes are still in our own hands and that we hold the power to save the future, that I feel the duty to speak out now that I have the occasion and the opportunity to do so. I do not believe that Soviet Russia desires war. What they desire is the fruits of war and the indefinite expansion of their power and doctrines. But what we have to consider here today while time remains, is the permanent prevention of war and the establishment of conditions of freedom and democracy as rapidly as possible in all countries. Our difficulties and dangers will not be removed by closing our eyes to them. They will not be removed by mere waiting to see what happens; nor will they be removed by a policy of appeasement. What is needed is a settlement, and the longer this is delayed, the more difficult it will be and the greater our dangers will become.

From what I have seen of our Russian friends and Allies during the war, I am convinced that there is nothing for which they have less respect than for weakness, especially military weakness. For that reason the old doctrine of a balance of power is unsound. We cannot afford, if we can help it, to work on narrow margins, offering temptations to a trial of strength. If the Western Democracies stand together in strict adherence to the principles of the United Nations Charter, their influence for furthering those principles will be immense and no one is likely to molest them. If however they become divided or falter in their duty and if these all-important years are allowed to slip away then indeed catastrophe may overwhelm us all.

Last time I saw it all coming and I cried aloud to my own fellow-countrymen and to the world, but no one paid any attention. Up till the year 1933 or even 1935, Germany might have been saved from the awful fate which has overtaken her and we might all have been spared the miseries Hitler let loose upon mankind. There never was a war in history easier to prevent by timely action than the one which has just desolated such great areas of the globe. It could have been prevented in my belief without the firing of a single shot, and Germany might be powerful, prosperous and honored today; but no one would listen and one by one we were all sucked into the awful whirlpool. We surely, ladies and gentlemen, I put it to you, surely, we must not let it happen again. This can only be achieved by reaching now, in 1946, by reaching a good understanding on all points with Russia under the general authority of the United Nations Organization and by the maintenance of that good understanding through many peaceful years, by the whole strength of the English-speaking world and all its connections. There is the solution which I respectfully offer to you in this Address to which I have given the title, "The Sinews of Peace".

Let no man underrate the abiding power of the British Empire and Commonwealth. Because you see the 46 millions in our island harassed about their food supply, of which they only grow one half, even in war-time, or because we have difficulty in restarting our industries and export trade after six years of passionate war effort, do not suppose we shall not come through these dark years of privation as we have come through the glorious years of agony. Do not suppose that half a century from now you will not see 70 or 80 millions of Britons spread about the world united in defense of our traditions, and our way of life, and of the world causes which you and we espouse. If the population of the English-speaking Commonwealths be added to that of the United States with all that such co-operation implies in the air, on the sea, all over the globe and in science and in industry, and in moral force,

there will be no quivering, precarious balance of power to offer its temptation to ambition or adventure. On the contrary there will be an overwhelming assurance of security. If we adhere faithfully to the Charter of the United Nations and walk forward in sedate and sober strength seeking no one's land or treasure, seeking to lay no arbitrary control upon the thoughts of men; if all British moral and material forces and convictions are joined with your own in fraternal association, the highroads of the future will be clear, not only for our time, but for a century to come.

Winston Churchill, Franklin Roosevelt, Josef Stalin, and others in Yalta, U.S.S.R., February 9, 1945

Evil Empire Speech
by Ronald Reagan (March 8, 1983)

President Roland Reagan delivered a wide-ranging speech to a meeting of the National Association of Evangelicals (NAE) in March of 1983. It is best known for his reference to the Soviet Union as an "evil empire," but it makes a powerful case for Biblical stances on many issues. At the time, Congress was considering a proposal for a nuclear freeze, which would have prevented the Reagan Administration from deploying nuclear missiles in Europe. Reagan opposed the freeze, and he decided to use part of his NAE speech to explain his position. Many in the American media and many of Reagan's political opponents were appalled at the reference to the Soviet Union; but when imprisoned political dissidents in Russia heard about it, they were heartened that someone had finally told the truth about the system that had put them in prison for their thoughts.

Reverend clergy all, Senator Hawkins, distinguished members of the Florida congressional delegation, and all of you:

I can't tell you how you have warmed my heart with your welcome. I'm delighted to be here today. Those of you in the National Association of Evangelicals are known for your spiritual and humanitarian work. And I would be especially remiss if I didn't discharge right now one personal debt of gratitude. Thank you for your prayers. Nancy and I have felt their presence many times in many ways. And believe me, for us they've made all the difference.

The other day in the East Room of the White House at a meeting there, someone asked me whether I was aware of all the people out there who were praying for the President. And I had to say, "Yes, I am. I've felt it. I believe in intercessionary prayer."

President Ronald Reagan at the 41st Annual Convention of the National Association of Evangelicals

But I couldn't help but say to that questioner after he'd asked the question that—or at least say to them that if sometimes when he was praying he got a busy signal, it was just me in there ahead of him. [Laughter] I think I understand how Abraham Lincoln felt when he said, "I have been driven many times to my knees by the overwhelming conviction that I had nowhere else to go."

From the joy and the good feeling of this conference, I go to a political reception. [Laughter]

Now, I don't know why, but that bit of scheduling reminds me of a story—[laughter]—which I'll share with you.

An evangelical minister and a politician arrived at Heaven's gate one day together. And St. Peter, after doing all the necessary formalities, took them in hand to show them where their quarters would be. And he took them to a small, single room with a bed, a chair, and a table and said this was for the clergyman. And the politician was a little worried about what might be in store for him. And he couldn't believe it then when St. Peter stopped in front of a beautiful mansion with lovely grounds, many servants, and told him that these would be his quarters.

And he couldn't help but ask, he said, "But wait, how—there's something wrong—how do I get this mansion while that good and holy man only gets a single room?" And St. Peter said, "You have to understand how things are up here. We've got thousands and thousands of clergy. You're the first politician who ever made it." [Laughter]

But I don't want to contribute to a stereotype. [Laughter] So, I tell you there are a great many God-fearing, dedicated, noble men and women in public life, present company included. And yes, we need your help to keep us ever mindful of the ideas and the principles that brought us into the public arena in the first place. The basis of those ideals and principles is a commitment to freedom and personal liberty that, itself, is grounded in the much deeper realization that freedom prospers only where the blessings of God are avidly sought and humbly accepted.

The American experiment in democracy rests on this insight. Its discovery was the great triumph of our Founding Fathers, voiced by William Penn when he said, "If we will not be governed by God, we must be governed by tyrants." Explaining the inalienable rights of men, Jefferson said, "The God who gave us life, gave us liberty at the same time." And it was George Washington who said that "of all the dispositions and habits which lead to political prosperity, religion and morality are indispensable supports."

And finally, that shrewdest of all observers of American democracy, Alexis de Tocqueville, put it eloquently after he had gone on a search for the secret of America's greatness and genius—and he said, "Not until I went into the churches of America and heard her pulpits aflame with righteousness did I understand the greatness and the genius of America. America is great because America is good. And if America ever ceases to be good, America will cease to be great."

Well, I'm pleased to be here today with you who are keeping America great by keeping her good. Only through your work and prayers and those of millions of others can we hope to survive this perilous century and keep alive this experiment in liberty—this last, best hope of man.

I want you to know that this administration is motivated by a political philosophy that sees the greatness of America in you, her people, and in your families, churches, neighborhoods, communities—the institutions that foster and nourish values like concern for others and respect for the rule of law under God.

Now, I don't have to tell you that this puts us in opposition to, or at least out of step with, a prevailing attitude of many who have turned to a modern-day secularism, discarding the tried and time-tested values upon which our very civilization is based. No matter how well intentioned, their value system is radically different from that of most Americans. And while they proclaim that they're freeing us from superstitions of the past, they've taken upon themselves the job of superintending us by government rule and regulation. Sometimes their voices are louder than ours, but they are not yet a majority.

An example of that vocal superiority is evident in a controversy now going on in Washington. And since I'm involved, I've been waiting to hear from the parents of young America. How far are they willing to go in giving to government their prerogatives as parents?

Let me state the case as briefly and simply as I can. An organization of citizens, sincerely motivated and deeply concerned about the increase in illegitimate births and abortions involving girls well below the age of consent, sometime ago established a nationwide network of clinics to offer help to these girls and, hopefully, alleviate this situation. Now, again, let me say, I do not fault their intent. However, in their well-intentioned effort, these clinics have decided to provide advice and birth control drugs and devices to underage girls without the knowledge of their parents.

For some years now, the federal government has helped with funds to subsidize these clinics. In providing for this, the Congress decreed that every effort would be made to maximize parental participation. Nevertheless, the drugs and devices are prescribed without getting parental consent or giving notification after they've done so. Girls termed "sexually active"—and that has replaced the word "promiscuous"—are given this help in order to prevent illegitimate birth or abortion.

Well, we have ordered clinics receiving federal funds to notify the parents such help has been given. One of the nation's leading newspapers has created the term "squeal rule" in editorializing against us for doing this, and we're being criticized for violating the privacy of young people. A judge has recently granted an injunction against an enforcement of our rule. I've watched TV panel shows discuss this issue, seen columnists pontificating on our error, but no one seems to mention morality as playing a part in the subject of sex.

Is all of Judeo-Christian tradition wrong? Are we to believe that something so sacred can be looked upon as a purely physical thing with no potential for emotional and psychological harm? And isn't it the parents' right to give counsel and advice to keep their children from making mistakes that may affect their entire lives?

Many of us in government would like to know what parents think about this intrusion in their family by government. We're going to fight in the courts. The right of parents and the rights of family take precedence over those of Washington-based bureaucrats and social engineers.

But the fight against parental notification is really only one example of many attempts to water down traditional values and even abrogate the original terms of American democracy. Freedom prospers when religion is vibrant and the rule of law under God is acknowledged. When our Founding Fathers passed the First Amendment, they sought to protect churches from government interference. They never intended to construct a wall of hostility between government and the concept of religious belief itself.

The evidence of this permeates our history and our government. The Declaration of Independence mentions the Supreme Being no less than four times. "In God We Trust" is engraved on our coinage. The Supreme Court opens its proceedings with a religious invocation. And the members of Congress open their sessions with a prayer. I just happen to believe the schoolchildren of the United States are entitled to the same privileges as Supreme Court Justices and Congressmen.

Last year, I sent the Congress a constitutional amendment to restore prayer to public schools. Already this session, there's growing bipartisan support for the amendment, and I am calling on the Congress to act speedily to pass it and to let our children pray.

Perhaps some of you read recently about the Lubbock school case, where a judge actually ruled that it was unconstitutional for a school district to give equal treatment to religious and nonreligious student groups, even when the group meetings were being held during the students' own time. The First Amendment never intended to require government to discriminate against religious speech.

Senators Denton and Hatfield have proposed legislation in the Congress on the whole question of prohibiting discrimination against religious forms of student speech. Such legislation could go far to restore freedom of religious speech for public school students. And I hope the Congress considers these bills quickly. And with your help, I think it's possible we could also get the constitutional amendment through the Congress this year.

More than a decade ago, a Supreme Court decision literally wiped off the books of 50 States statutes protecting the rights of unborn children. Abortion on demand now takes the lives of up to one and a half million unborn children a year. Human life legislation ending this tragedy will some day pass the Congress, and you and I must never rest until it does. Unless and until it can be proven that the unborn child is not a living entity, then its right to life, liberty, and the pursuit of happiness must be protected.

You may remember that when abortion on demand began, many, and, indeed, I'm sure many of you, warned that the practice would lead to a decline in respect for human life, that the philosophical premises used to justify abortion on demand would ultimately be used to justify other attacks on the sacredness of human life—infanticide or mercy killing. Tragically enough, those warnings proved all too true. Only last year a court permitted the death by starvation of a handicapped infant.

I have directed the Health and Human Services Department to make clear to every health care facility in the United States that the Rehabilitation Act of 1973 protects all handicapped persons against discrimination based on handicaps, including infants. And we have taken the further step of requiring that each and every recipient of Federal funds who provides health care services to infants must post and keep posted in a conspicuous place a notice stating that "discriminatory failure to feed and care for handicapped infants in this facility is prohibited by Federal law." It also lists a 24-hour, toll-free number so that nurses and others may report violations in time to save the infant's life.

In addition, recent legislation introduced in the Congress by Representative Henry Hyde of Illinois not only increases restrictions on publicly financed abortions, it also addresses this whole problem of infanticide. I urge the Congress to begin hearings and to adopt legislation that will protect the right of life to all children, including the disabled or handicapped.

Now, I'm sure that you must get discouraged at times, but you've done better than you know, perhaps. There's a great spiritual awakening in America, a renewal of the traditional values that have been the bedrock of America's goodness and greatness.

One recent survey by a Washington-based research council concluded that Americans were far more religious than the people of other nations; 95 percent of those surveyed expressed a belief in God and a huge majority believed the Ten Commandments had real meaning in their lives. And another study has found that an overwhelming majority of Americans disapprove of adultery, teenage sex, pornography, abortion, and hard drugs. And this same study showed a deep reverence for the importance of family ties and religious belief.

I think the items that we've discussed here today must be a key part of the Nation's political agenda. For the first time the Congress is openly and seriously debating and dealing with the prayer and abortion issues—and that's enormous progress right there. I repeat: America is in the midst of a spiritual awakening and a moral renewal. And with your Biblical keynote, I say today, "Yes, let justice roll on like a river, righteousness like a never-failing stream."

Now, obviously, much of this new political and social consensus I've talked about is based on a positive view of American history, one that takes pride in our country's accomplishments and record. But we must never forget that no government schemes are going to perfect man. We know that living in this world means dealing with what philosophers would call the phenomenology of evil or, as theologians would put it, the doctrine of sin.

There is sin and evil in the world, and we're enjoined by Scripture and the Lord Jesus to oppose it with all our might. Our nation, too, has a legacy of evil with which it must deal. The glory of this land has been its capacity for transcending the moral evils of our past. For example, the long struggle of minority citizens for equal rights, once a source of disunity and civil war, is now a point of pride for all Americans. We must never go back. There is no room for racism, anti-Semitism, or other forms of ethnic and racial hatred in this country.

I know that you've been horrified, as have I, by the resurgence of some hate groups preaching bigotry and prejudice. Use the mighty voice of your pulpits and the powerful standing of your churches to denounce and isolate these hate groups in our midst. The commandment given us is clear and simple: "Thou shalt love thy neighbor as thyself."

But whatever sad episodes exist in our past, any objective observer must hold a positive view of American history, a history that has been the story of hopes fulfilled and dreams made into reality. Especially in this century, America has kept alight the torch of freedom, but not just for ourselves but for millions of others around the world.

And this brings me to my final point today. During my first press conference as President, in answer to a direct question, I pointed out that, as good Marxist-Leninists, the Soviet leaders have openly and publicly declared that the only morality they recognize is that which will further their cause, which is world revolution. I think I should point out I was only quoting Lenin, their guiding spirit, who said in 1920 that they repudiate all morality that proceeds from supernatural ideas—that's their name for religion—or ideas that are outside class conceptions. Morality is entirely subordinate to the interests of class war. And everything is moral that is necessary for the annihilation of the old, exploiting social order and for uniting the proletariat.

Well, I think the refusal of many influential people to accept this elementary fact of Soviet doctrine illustrates an historical reluctance to see totalitarian powers for what they are. We saw this phenomenon in the 1930's. We see it too often today.

U.S.S.R.
Postage Stamp

This doesn't mean we should isolate ourselves and refuse to seek an understanding with them. I intend to do everything I can to persuade them of our peaceful intent, to remind them that it was the West that refused to use its nuclear monopoly in the forties and fifties for territorial gain and which now proposes a 50-percent cut in strategic ballistic missiles and the elimination of an entire class of land-based, intermediate-range nuclear missiles.

At the same time, however, they must be made to understand we will never compromise our principles and standards. We will never give away our freedom. We will never abandon our belief in God. And we will never stop searching for a genuine peace. But we can assure none of these things America stands for through the so-called nuclear freeze solutions proposed by some. The truth is that a freeze now would be a very dangerous fraud, for that is merely the illusion of peace. The reality is that we must find peace through strength.

I would agree to a freeze if only we could freeze the Soviets' global desires. A freeze at current levels of weapons would remove any incentive for the Soviets to negotiate seriously in Geneva and virtually end our chances to achieve the major arms reductions which we have proposed. Instead, they would achieve their objectives through the freeze.

A freeze would reward the Soviet Union for its enormous and unparalleled military buildup. It would prevent the essential and long overdue modernization of United States and allied defenses and would leave our aging forces increasingly vulnerable. And an honest freeze would require extensive prior negotiations on the systems and numbers to be limited and on the measures to ensure effective verification and compliance. And the kind of a freeze that has been suggested would be virtually impossible to verify. Such a major effort would divert us completely from our current negotiations on achieving substantial reductions.

A number of years ago, I heard a young father, a very prominent young man in the entertainment world, addressing a tremendous gathering in California. It was during the time of the Cold War, and communism and our own way of life were very much on people's minds. And he was speaking to that subject. And suddenly, though, I heard him saying, "I love my little girls more than anything—"

And I said to myself, "Oh, no, don't. You can't—don't say that."

But I had underestimated him. He went on: "I would rather see my little girls die now, still believing in God, than have them grow up under communism and one day die no longer believing in God."

There were thousands of young people in that audience. They came to their feet with shouts of joy. They had instantly recognized the profound truth in what he had said, with regard to the physical and the soul and what was truly important.

Yes, let us pray for the salvation of all of those who live in that totalitarian darkness—pray they will discover the joy of knowing God. But until they do, let us be aware that while they preach the supremacy of the state, declare its omnipotence over individual man, and predict its eventual domination of all peoples on the Earth, they are the focus of evil in the modern world.

It was C. S. Lewis who, in his unforgettable *Screwtape Letters*, wrote: "The greatest evil is not done now in those sordid 'dens of crime' that Dickens loved to paint. It is not even done in concentration camps and labor camps. In those we see its final result. But it is conceived and ordered (moved, seconded, carried and minuted) in clear, carpeted, warmed, and well-lighted offices, by quiet men with white collars and cut fingernails and smooth-shaven cheeks who do not need to raise their voice."

Well, because these "quiet men" do not "raise their voices"; because they sometimes speak in soothing tones of brotherhood and peace; because, like other dictators before them, they're always making "their final territorial demand," some would have us accept them at their word and accommodate ourselves to their aggressive impulses. But if history teaches anything, it teaches that simple-minded appeasement or wishful thinking about our adversaries is folly. It means the betrayal of our past, the squandering of our freedom.

So, I urge you to speak out against those who would place the United States in a position of military and moral inferiority. You know, I've always believed that old Screwtape reserved his best efforts for those of you in the church. So, in your discussions of the nuclear freeze proposals, I urge you to beware the temptation of pride—the temptation of blithely declaring yourselves above it all and label both sides equally at fault, to ignore the facts of history and the aggressive impulses of an evil empire, to simply call the arms race a giant misunderstanding and thereby remove yourself from the struggle between right and wrong and good and evil.

I ask you to resist the attempts of those who would have you withhold your support for our efforts, this administration's efforts, to keep America strong and free, while we negotiate real and verifiable reductions in the world's nuclear arsenals and one day, with God's help, their total elimination.

While America's military strength is important, let me add here that I've always maintained that the struggle now going on for the world will never be decided by bombs or rockets, by armies or military might. The real crisis we face today is a spiritual one; at root, it is a test of moral will and faith.

Whittaker Chambers, the man whose own religious conversion made him a witness to one of the terrible traumas of our time, the Hiss-Chambers case, wrote that the crisis of the Western World exists to the degree in which the West is indifferent to God, the degree to which it collaborates in communism's attempt to make man stand alone without God. And then he said, for Marxism-Leninism is actually the second oldest faith, first proclaimed in the Garden of Eden with the words of temptation, "Ye shall be as gods."

The Western world can answer this challenge, he wrote, "but only provided that its faith in God and the freedom He enjoins is as great as communism's faith in Man."

I believe we shall rise to the challenge. I believe that communism is another sad, bizarre chapter in human history whose last pages even now are being written. I believe this because the source of our strength in the quest for human freedom is not material, but spiritual. And because it knows no limitation, it must terrify and ultimately triumph over those who would enslave their fellow man. For in the words of Isaiah: "He giveth power to the faint; and to them that have no might He increased strength. But they that wait upon the Lord shall renew their strength; they shall mount up with wings as eagles; they shall run, and not be weary."

Yes, change your world. One of our Founding Fathers, Thomas Paine, said, "We have it within our power to begin the world over again." We can do it, doing together what no one church could do by itself.

President Ronald Reagan

God bless you, and thank you very much.

"Mr. Gorbachev, Tear Down This Wall!"
Speech by Ronald Reagan (June 12, 1987)

*After six and one-half years in office, President Ronald Reagan gave this speech
while visiting Berlin, Germany. He was standing near the wall
that had separated East and West Berlin for over a quarter of a century.*

*President Reagan during his speech
in front of the Brandenburg Gate*

Chancellor Kohl, Governing Mayor Diepgen, ladies and gentlemen: Twenty-four years ago, President John F. Kennedy visited Berlin, speaking to the people of this city and the world at the City Hall. Well, since then two other presidents have come, each in his turn, to Berlin. And today I, myself, make my second visit to your city.

We come to Berlin, we American presidents, because it's our duty to speak, in this place, of freedom. But I must confess, we're drawn here by other things as well: by the feeling of history in this city, more than 500 years older than our own nation; by the beauty of the Grunewald and the Tiergarten; most of all, by your courage and determination. Perhaps the composer Paul Lincke understood something about American presidents. You see, like so many presidents before me, I come here today because wherever I go, whatever I do: Ich hab noch einen Koffer in Berlin. [I still have a suitcase in Berlin.]

Our gathering today is being broadcast throughout Western Europe and North America. I understand that it is being seen and heard as well in the East. To those listening throughout Eastern Europe, a special word: Although I cannot be with you, I address my remarks to you just as surely as to those standing here before me. For I join you, as I join your fellow countrymen in the West, in this firm, this unalterable belief: Es gibt nur ein Berlin. [There is only one Berlin.]

Behind me stands a wall that encircles the free sectors of this city, part of a vast system of barriers that divides the entire continent of Europe. From the Baltic, south, those barriers cut across Germany in a gash of barbed wire, concrete, dog runs, and guard towers. Farther south, there may be no visible, no obvious wall. But there remain armed guards and checkpoints all the same—still a restriction on the right to travel, still an instrument to impose upon ordinary men and women the will of a totalitarian state. Yet it is here in Berlin where the wall emerges most clearly; here, cutting across your city, where the news photo and the television screen have imprinted this brutal division of a continent upon the mind of the world. Standing before the Brandenburg Gate, every man is a German, separated from his fellow men. Every man is a Berliner, forced to look upon a scar.

President von Weizsacker has said, "The German question is open as long as the Brandenburg Gate is closed." Today I say: As long as the gate is closed, as long as this scar of a wall is permitted to stand, it is not the German question alone that remains open, but the question of freedom for all mankind. Yet I do not come here to lament. For I find in Berlin a message of hope, even in the shadow of this wall, a message of triumph.

In this season of spring in 1945, the people of Berlin emerged from their air-raid shelters to find devastation. Thousands of miles away, the people of the United States reached out to help. And in 1947 Secretary of State—as you've been told—George Marshall announced the creation of what would become known as the Marshall Plan. Speaking precisely 40 years ago this month, he said: "Our policy is directed not against any country or doctrine, but against hunger, poverty, desperation, and chaos."

In the Reichstag a few moments ago, I saw a display commemorating this 40th anniversary of the Marshall Plan. I was struck by the sign on a burnt-out, gutted structure that was being rebuilt. I understand that Berliners of my own generation can remember seeing signs like it dotted throughout the western sectors of the city. The sign read simply: "The Marshall Plan is helping here to strengthen the free world." A strong, free world in the West, that dream became real. Japan rose from ruin to become an economic giant. Italy, France, Belgium— virtually every nation in Western Europe saw political and economic rebirth; the European Community was founded.

The Berlin Wall

In West Germany and here in Berlin, there took place an economic miracle, the Wirtschaftswunder. Adenauer, Erhard, Reuter, and other leaders understood the practical importance of liberty—that just as truth can flourish only when the journalist is given freedom of speech, so prosperity can come about only when the farmer and businessman enjoy economic freedom. The German leaders reduced tariffs, expanded free trade, lowered taxes. From 1950 to 1960 alone, the standard of living in West Germany and Berlin doubled.

Where four decades ago there was rubble, today in West Berlin there is the greatest industrial output of any city in Germany—busy office blocks, fine homes and apartments, proud avenues, and the spreading lawns of parkland. Where a city's culture seemed to have been destroyed, today there are two great universities, orchestras and an opera, countless theaters, and museums. Where there was want, today there's abundance—food, clothing, automobiles—the wonderful goods of the Ku'damm. From devastation, from utter ruin, you

Reagan on speaker's platform, Berlin, Germany

Berliners have, in freedom, rebuilt a city that once again ranks as one of the greatest on earth. The Soviets may have had other plans. But my friends, there were a few things the Soviets didn't count on—Berliner Herz, Berliner Humor, ja, und Berliner Schnauze. [Berliner heart, Berliner humor, yes, and a Berliner Schnauze.]

In the 1950s, Khrushchev predicted: "We will bury you." But in the West today, we see a free world that has achieved a level of prosperity and well-being unprecedented in all human history. In the Communist world, we see failure, technological backwardness, declining standards of health, even want of the most basic kind—too little food. Even today, the Soviet Union still cannot feed itself. After these four decades, then, there stands before the entire world one great and inescapable conclusion: Freedom leads to prosperity. Freedom replaces the ancient hatreds among the nations with comity and peace. Freedom is the victor.

And now the Soviets themselves may, in a limited way, be coming to understand the importance of freedom. We hear much from Moscow about a new policy of reform and openness. Some political prisoners have been released. Certain foreign news broadcasts are no longer being jammed. Some economic enterprises have been permitted to operate with greater freedom from state control.

Are these the beginnings of profound changes in the Soviet state? Or are they token gestures, intended to raise false hopes in the West, or to strengthen the Soviet system without changing it? We welcome change and openness; for we believe that freedom and security go together, that the advance of human liberty can only strengthen the cause of world peace. There is one sign the Soviets can make that would be unmistakable, that would advance dramatically the cause of freedom and peace.

General Secretary Gorbachev, if you seek peace, if you seek prosperity for the Soviet Union and Eastern Europe, if you seek liberalization: Come here to this gate! Mr. Gorbachev, open this gate! Mr. Gorbachev, tear down this wall!

I understand the fear of war and the pain of division that afflict this continent—and I pledge to you my country's efforts to help overcome these burdens. To be sure, we in the West must resist Soviet expansion. So we must maintain defenses of unassailable strength. Yet we seek peace; so we must strive to reduce arms on both sides.

Beginning 10 years ago, the Soviets challenged the Western alliance with a grave new threat, hundreds of new and more deadly SS-20 nuclear missiles, capable of striking every capital in Europe. The Western alliance responded by committing itself to a counter-deployment unless the Soviets agreed to negotiate a better solution; namely, the elimination of such weapons on both sides. For many months, the Soviets refused to bargain in earnestness. As the alliance, in turn, prepared to go forward with its counter-deployment, there were difficult days—days of protests like those during my 1982 visit to this city—and the Soviets later walked away from the table.

But through it all, the alliance held firm. And I invite those who protested then—I invite those who protest today—to mark this fact: Because we remained strong, the Soviets came back to the table. And because we remained strong, today we have within reach the possibility, not merely of limiting the growth of arms, but of eliminating, for the first time, an entire class of nuclear weapons from the face of the earth.

NATO Flag

As I speak, NATO ministers are meeting in Iceland to review the progress of our proposals for eliminating these weapons. At the talks in Geneva, we have also proposed deep cuts in strategic offensive weapons. And the Western allies have likewise made far-reaching proposals to reduce the danger of conventional war and to place a total ban on chemical weapons.

While we pursue these arms reductions, I pledge to you that we will maintain the capacity to deter Soviet aggression at any level at which it might occur. And in cooperation with many of our allies, the United States is pursuing the Strategic Defense Initiative—research to base deterrence not on the threat of offensive retaliation, but on defenses that truly defend; on systems, in short, that will not target populations, but shield them. By these means we seek to increase the safety of Europe and all the world. But we must remember a crucial fact: East and West do not mistrust each other because we are armed; we are armed because we mistrust each other. And our differences are not about weapons but about liberty. When President Kennedy spoke at the City Hall those 24 years ago, freedom was encircled, Berlin was under siege. And today, despite all the pressures upon this city, Berlin stands secure in its liberty. And freedom itself is transforming the globe.

In the Philippines, in South and Central America, democracy has been given a rebirth. Throughout the Pacific, free markets are working miracle after miracle of economic growth. In the industrialized nations, a technological revolution is taking place—a revolution marked by rapid, dramatic advances in computers and telecommunications.

In Europe, only one nation and those it controls refuse to join the community of freedom. Yet in this age of redoubled economic growth, of information and innovation, the Soviet Union faces a choice: It must make fundamental changes, or it will become obsolete.

Today thus represents a moment of hope. We in the West stand ready to cooperate with the East to promote true openness, to break down barriers that separate people, to create a safe, freer world. And surely there is no better place than Berlin, the meeting place of East and West, to make a start. Free people of Berlin: Today, as in the past, the United States stands for the strict observance and full implementation of all parts of the Four Power Agreement of 1971. Let us use this occasion, the 750th anniversary of this city, to usher in a new era, to seek a still fuller, richer life for the Berlin of the future. Together, let us maintain and develop the ties between the Federal Republic and the Western sectors of Berlin, which is permitted by the 1971 agreement.

And I invite Mr. Gorbachev: Let us work to bring the Eastern and Western parts of the city closer together, so that all the inhabitants of all Berlin can enjoy the benefits that come with life in one of the great cities of the world.

To open Berlin still further to all Europe, East and West, let us expand the vital air access to this city, finding ways of making commercial air service to Berlin more convenient, more comfortable, and more economical. We look to the day when West Berlin can become one of the chief aviation hubs in all central Europe.

With our French and British partners, the United States is prepared to help bring international meetings to Berlin. It would be only fitting for Berlin to serve as the site of United Nations meetings, or world conferences on human rights and arms control or other issues that call for international cooperation.

*Reichstag – Home of
The German Parliament*

There is no better way to establish hope for the future than to enlighten young minds, and we would be honored to sponsor summer youth exchanges, cultural events, and other programs for young Berliners from the East. Our French and British friends, I'm certain, will do the same. And it's my hope that an authority can be found in East Berlin to sponsor visits from young people of the Western sectors.

One final proposal, one close to my heart: Sport represents a source of enjoyment and ennoblement, and you may have noted that the Republic of Korea—South Korea—has offered to permit certain events of the 1988 Olympics to take place in the North. International sports competitions of all kinds could take place in both parts of this city. And what better way to demonstrate to the world the openness of this city than to offer in some future year to hold the Olympic games here in Berlin, East and West? In these four decades, as I have said, you Berliners have built a great city. You've done so in spite of threats—the Soviet attempts to impose the East-mark, the blockade. Today the city thrives in spite of the challenges implicit in the very presence of this wall. What keeps you here? Certainly there's a great deal to be said for your fortitude, for your defiant courage. But I believe there's something deeper, something that involves Berlin's whole look and feel and way of life—not mere sentiment. No one could live long in Berlin without being completely disabused of illusions. Something instead, that has seen the difficulties of life in Berlin but chose to accept them, that continues to build this good and proud city in contrast to a surrounding totalitarian presence that refuses to release human energies or aspirations. Something that speaks with a powerful voice of affirmation, that says yes to this city, yes to the future, yes to freedom. In a word, I would submit that what keeps you in Berlin is love—love both profound and abiding.

President Reagan

Perhaps this gets to the root of the matter, to the most fundamental distinction of all between East and West. The totalitarian world produces backwardness because it does such violence to the spirit, thwarting the human impulse to create, to enjoy, to worship. The totalitarian world finds even symbols of love and of worship an affront. Years ago, before the East Germans began rebuilding their churches, they erected a secular structure: the television tower at Alexander Platz. Virtually ever since, the authorities have been working to correct what they view as the tower's one major flaw, treating the glass sphere at the top with paints and chemicals of every kind. Yet even today when the sun strikes that sphere— that sphere that towers over all Berlin—the light makes the sign of the cross. There in Berlin, like the city itself, symbols of love, symbols of worship, cannot be suppressed.

As I looked out a moment ago from the Reichstag [the German parliament], that embodiment of German unity, I noticed words crudely spray-painted upon the wall, perhaps by a young Berliner: "This wall will fall. Beliefs become reality." Yes, across Europe, this wall will fall. For it cannot withstand faith; it cannot withstand truth. The wall cannot withstand freedom.

And I would like, before I close, to say one word. I have read, and I have been questioned since I've been here about certain demonstrations against my coming. And I would like to say just one thing, and to those who demonstrate so. I wonder if they have ever asked themselves that if they should have the kind of government they apparently seek, no one would ever be able to do what they're doing again.

Thank you and God bless you all.

Credits

We have attempted properly to use and attribute the texts and images in this book.
If you have any questions concerning them, please direct them to the publisher.

Documents

Extract from the Journal of Christopher Columbus. From the AmDocs section of CARRIE: A Full-Text Electronic Library. Accessed July 3, 2004. http://www.ku.edu/carrie/docs/texts/acolon.html

Extract from the Magna Carta. Prepared by Gerald Murphy and Nancy Troutman of The Cleveland Free-Net, a part of the National Public Telecomputing Network. Website of origin: www.constitution.org

Preface to *Philosophiae Naturalis Principia Mathematica.* Translated by Andrew Motte. Taken from Volume 39 of the Harvard Classics (pp. 157-159).

Where Love Is, God Is. Translated by L. and A. Maude, 1907. Source: Christian Classics Ethereal Library, Calvin College. www.ccel.org

Other Documents. Acquired from standard texts and public domain databases.

Images

Christian Theological Seminary Image Library 1
Cyber Hymnal (www.cyberhymnal.org) 29, 32, 34, 36, 42, 51, 75, 91, 93, 115, 125
Dover (Electronic) Clip Art Series 5, 16, 22, 31, 38-39
Franklin D. Roosevelt Library Digital Archives 168-173, 176-177
George Müller of Bristol (Republished by Kregel Publications, 1999) 143
JupiterImages cover, title, 2, 6-7, 9e, 10b, 13-15, 17-18, 20-21, 23-24, 26, 30, 33a, 37, 41, 43-50, 53, 55, 57, 60, 63, 66, 69-71, 72-74, 81, 83, 85-90, 97, 99, 101-102, 103, 105-111, 113-114, 117-120, 122-123, 126-133, 135-139, 141, 144-145, 146b, 147-150, 153-163, 165-167, 174, 179-184, 187, 189-190
Nova Development Corporation 8, 9a-d, 10a-c-d, 11-12, 19, 27-28, 33b, 35, 40, 76-80, 92, 94-96, 98, 100, 112, 116, 121, 124-125, 134, 146a, 151-152, 164
Reagan Library Archives 178, 185-186, 188, 191

Index of Authors

Index of Titles

Index of Subjects

Hymns

Poems

Short Stories and Fables

Also by Ray Notgrass

Exploring America

High school curriculum combining American history, American literature, and Bible. It helps high school students gain a fuller understanding of our nation's past as they read the history narrative, read classic American literature, complete writing assignments, and study what the Bible says about issues and ideas in American history.

Exploring Government

A complete, one-semester study for high school students about American Federal, state, and local government, with special emphasis on the U.S. Constitution. Package includes a collection of historical documents, speeches, and essays.

For information about these and other resources
available from the Notgrass Company,
call 1-800-211-8793 or visit www.notgrass.com.